The Devils' Gospels

Finding God in Four Great Atheist Books

The Devils' Gospels

Finding God in Four Great Atheist Books

By Christopher Gasson

CHRISTIAN ALTERNATIVE
BOOKS

London, UK
Washington, DC, USA

CollectiveInk

First published by Christian Alternative Books, 2025
Christian Alternative Books is an imprint of Collective Ink Ltd.,
Unit 11, Shepperton House, 89 Shepperton Road, London, N1 3DF
office@collectiveinkbooks.com
www.collectiveinkbooks.com
www.christian-alternative.com

For distributor details and how to order please visit the 'Ordering' section on our website.

Text copyright: Christopher Gasson 2023

ISBN: 978 1 80341 279 5
978 1 80341 280 1 (ebook)
Library of Congress Control Number: 2023948917

A CIP catalogue record for this book is available from the British Library.

Design: Lapiz Digital Services

UK: Printed and bound by CPI Group (UK) Ltd, Croydon, CR0 4YY
Printed in North America by CPI GPS partners

We operate a distinctive and ethical publishing philosophy in all areas of our business, from our global network of authors to production and worldwide distribution.

Contents

Acknowledgements

I would like to thank Jemima, Julius, Jerome, Aphra, Isidore, Clement, Rosie, Edith, Magnus, Maddie, Sammy, William, Josh, Katie, Eleanor, Esther and all those who attended the youth discussion group at the University Church. I would also like to thank Brian Mountford for his advice and assistance in developing the idea for the book; Alec Charles, Chris Bowling and Mantas Krisciunas for their expert input in the editing process; and my wife, Lucy, for her brilliance in discussion of the core ideas in the book as well as her forbearance during the writing process.

Chapter 1

Introduction: The Rebellion

How Can You Find God in These Four Great Atheist Books?

Can we read great atheist books as holy scripture? That is the question of this book.

It sounds like a provocation, but it has a logic to it. If God really is the great superlative, the Almighty, the ground of our being, then everything that anyone can say about life and the world should tell us more about God. That means we can find God even in works that are savagely opposed to God. Friedrich Nietzsche announces the death of God at the beginning of *Thus Spoke Zarathustra* and spends the rest of the book outlining his vision of self-realisation in the absence of God. Richard Dawkins wrote *The God Delusion* with the express objective of freeing people from the tyranny of religion. Jacques Derrida's *Writing and Difference* and Stephen Hawking's *A Brief History of Time* are equally challenging books from a religious perspective. Yet all of these books, if we read them carefully, can tell us things that we didn't know about the nature of God. The authors may believe they have done away with the divine, but they are betrayed by their writing. This book aims to explain how.

This is not just a perverse form of literary criticism; there is an urgency to this project. The Church sits on a burning platform. That is a business metaphor for a situation where there are no good outcomes, but you are forced to make an immediate decision. It refers to the horrific Piper Alpha disaster in 1988, when a North Sea oil production platform caught fire. Workers faced the choice of either staying put, in hope of rescue, or throwing themselves into the sea and hoping not to die of hypothermia before help arrived. The flames which are consuming Christianity are the flames of the culture war. The ice-cold sea is scepticism and atheism. One or the other will consume the Church if it does not act.

The culture war is killing Christianity from within. Religion and culture are deeply intertwined. For centuries it was a symbiotic relationship: religion reinforced culture and culture reinforced religion. Today it is becoming a destructive relationship. We now live in a world where culture is no longer defined by geography. Thanks to colonialism and immigration, people with different ideals live together side by side as they never did before. Instead of culture and religion working together to provide a sense of belonging for the whole community, they conspire to create a new sense of division. It is made worse by politicians such as Donald Trump and Vladimir Putin using religion to maximise their nativist appeal.

These political leaders are corrupting Christianity and betraying its values. Neither Trump nor Putin have the slightest interest in living the values expressed by the life and teachings of Jesus. Yet they both see in religion access to a passionate political base which, if activated, will support them through right or wrong. Some Church leaders are willing to facilitate that activation; it gives them a sense of power and relevance. Patriarch Kirill, who is head of the Russian Orthodox Church, has been a vocal supporter of Putin's war in Ukraine. He said that fighting for Russia 'washes away all sins'.[1] Meanwhile in the US, conservative Church leaders queue up to support Trump's politics. For example, Robert Jeffress, who is the pastor of the First Baptist Dallas Church, a Texas megachurch, went on Fox News in 2019 to provide the religious justification for building the border wall to keep out immigrants from Mexico. 'The Bible says even Heaven itself is gonna have a wall around it. Not everybody is going to be allowed in. So if walls are immoral, then God is immoral.'[2] Jeffress seems to have forgotten Matthew 25:35. That verse is unambiguous about how to treat refugees: 'I was hungry and you gave me something to eat, I was thirsty and you gave me something to drink, I was a stranger and you invited me in'. As Christianity allows itself to be taken over by nativist politics, the fundamentalists begin to forget the fundamentals. Scripture becomes a vehicle for political prejudice rather than an exploration of the will of God.

That is what is happening to the conservative side of the Church. It has become the tool of cynical politicians who do not care how much they debase it. But the fate of the liberal Church has been much worse.

That is because young people increasingly see a contradiction between being liberal and being Christian. Given the choice they prefer to identify as liberals rather than Christians. Liberalism is an important social value for young people growing up in diverse communities. Tolerating different faiths is part of that, but it doesn't sit well with the notion that there is one Christian God. Furthermore, liberal Church leaders give very little guidance on how to resolve this dilemma. They feel uncomfortable suggesting that there is only one true religion and everyone else is going to hell (as conservative Church leaders might). They also feel uncomfortable saying that there is nothing special about Christianity. The result is silence and young people make up their minds by looking around at what is happening globally. They see that many conflicts around the world are driven by religious intolerance and many of the loudest voices of bigotry are those of people who claim to be religious. They also look around at their friends and see that none of them need Christianity in order to be good people.

Does this mean that the destiny of Christianity is irrelevance? Will it be consumed by the secular liberalism of the left and the amoral political populism of the right, leaving no space for a God of love in between?

The purpose of this book is to show that there is a third alternative. Paradoxically the place to look for it is in the writings of those most opposed to the existence of God.

Where I Am Coming From

For me, being a Christian is a rebellion against irrelevance.

If you want to understand what it feels like, look at Goya's painting, *The Third of May 1808*. I have put a black and white version of it at the beginning of this chapter. It shows Spaniards arrested during the uprising against Napoleon's troops, an event that led to the Peninsular War. They are being executed in batches by a firing squad, according to Marshall Murat's orders. On the bottom left lie the corpses of the earlier victims; in the centre the next group hide their faces from their inevitable fate. Between these two groups, and in front of the faceless riflemen levelling their weapons, kneel six prisoners captured by Goya in the instant before they are to die. Among them, captured in a brilliant light to form the focus of the painting, is a man wearing a white shirt and yellow trousers. Outrage burns in his eyes as he throws his arms out in defiance. Death is inevitable. Others around him (including a monk) cower in acceptance. But the man in the white shirt will not go gently. It is as if he is trying to say, 'No, you've made a mistake. It can't be allowed to happen to me'. It is as if he is not just pleading for his life, but his whole existence. In an instant his whole life will become meaningless, but he refuses to accept that fate.

This rebellion is not just against death. It is also against life. The one exposes the futility of the other, and the more futile it looks, the stronger the instinct to rebel.

I'm happy to accept that my rebellion could be one of hope over logic. But that knowledge doesn't change my mind. In fact, it makes my resolve stronger. That is because this hope I feel seems to be something that cannot so easily be explained by logic. The fact that I have such a capacity for it suggests to me that there might be more to life that the bare facts of physics and biology might lead me to believe.

Hope doesn't provide me with better answers. What it does do is make me see more mystery in life. Why do we have this yearning for purpose, for connection, for beauty, for truth, for completeness? Furthermore, the mystery seems to grow the more we open our minds to it. It is difficult to describe. I suspect deliberately so. If I could articulate it fully, it would stop being a mystery. It would become a fact of life and I would lose interest.

For me the story that seems to speak most clearly to this mystery is the Christian story. In the life and teachings of Jesus, the cause of the mystery of life is love. I am using the word 'cause' in two senses here. Love is the cause in the sense that it is what makes us exist to experience life. It is also the cause in the sense that it is the objective that us rebels are invited to rally around. The process of trying to understand this love and make its cause my cause brings an incredible sense of richness to life, even though I am hopeless at following its ideal.

This richness is also the reason why I feel so strongly when I see Christianity hurtling towards its own irrelevance. Like the man in the white shirt, I want to shout, 'No, this is not how it is supposed to be!'

A University Church

The idea for this book grew out of a teenage discussion group that I used to run at the University Church of St Mary the Virgin in Oxford. My children were growing up and I wanted to keep them engaged with Christianity. Mostly when children turn 11, they stop coming to church. They are old enough to stay at home on their own if they want, and they have long grown out of the stories of Noah's Ark and Baby Jesus, which makes up the staple diet of Sunday schools. They don't find the liturgy of adult church engaging either. They have inquiring minds, but the format leaves no space for inquiry. Furthermore, it is very unlikely that any of their friends have to spend Sunday mornings in church. It means that in the back of their minds they are always asking questions like 'Why should I bother with any of this?' or 'Is a Christian something I want to be?'

The discussion group wasn't just for them, however. It was also for me. There is a terrible kind of icky piety that adults feel that they need to adopt when they talk to children about God. As a child it made me suspicious that ultimately there was something weak-minded about Christianity. The people who are supposed to teach you about God always seemed more concerned about not letting the side down, rather than saying what they really thought. They were rather over-enthusiastic about the platitudes and rather too quick to move on from the difficult questions. I longed to be able to ask someone, 'Why isn't this all rubbish?' and to challenge them at the first hint of mawkishness in their answer, but I never had the opportunity.

I stuck with Christianity, perhaps in part because I like to go against the grain. People like me — liberal, educated, logical, cynical — are supposed to be atheists. My hope was that by hanging in there it might eventually make more sense. Over time it did, but I still longed to have a decent no-holds-barred discussion about God with people who were quite happy to let the side down if it turned out to be nonsense. The teenagers in the University Church discussion group were the perfect foil.

We used to meet once a month during the Sunday service in the University Church's Old Library in Oxford. There is a symbolism in this which reflects the objective of this book. The room was built at a time — the 1320s — when learning about the world and learning about God were the same thing. A church that was a university and a university that was a church made total sense. Today the two are completely divided. There are no books in the Old Library anymore. Instead, its windows look out on the university's larger newer libraries (the Bodleian and the Radcliffe Camera), but the intellectual distance might be measured in lightyears. Religious thinking seems to exist in a totally separate solar system from secular thinking. It contributes to the sense of Christianity's growing irrelevance in the twenty-first century.

1860 and All That

This sense of irrelevance seems to have grown out of one of the central challenges of religion: how do you retain an eternal message in an ever-changing world? God is supposed to be timeless, but He or She has arranged a world which is in continuous flux. It means that as social mores change and our understanding of the world changes, there is an ever-growing challenge relating it to scripture. The instinct of the Church is to try to hold on to the past. That's why it was only in 1822 that the Catholic Church accepted that the earth rotated around the sun, and other denominations still struggle with the theory of evolution and the Big Bang. It is also why slavery, the subjugation of women, and homophobia were accepted by parts of the Church for longer than they have been by society at large. It means that while social change and the progress of science might be quite smoothly accelerating, the Church's recognition of this development happens in fits and starts, decades or even centuries in arrears.

As a result, churchgoers increasingly look like volunteer recruits for a time travel experiment, with different denominations selecting their decade of choice. (For the Amish it is the 1850s, while modish Anglicans prefer the 1980s. The 1950s are the decade of choice for most conservative evangelicals.) As the pace of social and technological change continues to pick up, there is a danger that the only adherents Christianity will be able to attract are refugees from modernity. Everyone else will scratch their heads and wonder what it is for.

It never had to be like that. I will explain why if you are prepared to join me for a few paragraphs in my own time travel machine. We are going back to Oxford in the year 1860. Two big things happened that year that changed the future of Christianity in England and possibly the world.

The first was the publication of a book entitled *Essays and Reviews* by a group of six learned clerics and one layman with strong Oxford connections. It was the brainchild of two former scholars of Balliol College: Frederick Temple (who went on to become Archbishop of Canterbury) and Benjamin Jowett (who was the Regius Professor of Greek at the university at the time). Both were excited by the implications of contemporary scholarship for Christianity and wanted the opportunity to explore them freely. As Jowett put it in a letter to the Regius Professor of Ecclesiastical History, Arthur Penrhyn Stanley, 'We do not wish to do anything rash or irritating to the public or the University, but we are determined not to submit to this abominable system of terrorism which prevents the statement of the plainest facts and makes true theology or theological education impossible'. [3]

On publication in March 1860, the book scandalised Victorian society and divided the Church of England. Samuel Wilberforce, the Bishop of Oxford, was so outraged by it that he campaigned for its authors to be tried for heresy in the Church courts. Two were found guilty but later acquitted when they appealed to the Privy Council (which is a secular court in the UK). A petition was then raised and signed by 137,000 lay members of the Church in opposition to the acquittal. Jowett found his £500 a year salary surreptitiously cut to £40 a year by the University. Temple found it necessary in 1870 to retract his contribution.

So what was it that the Church establishment found so very difficult? Mostly it was the idea that changing times meant changing views of the Bible. Temple's contribution, for example, suggested that individual conscience (and by extension, changing social mores) might take precedence over scripture: 'When conscience and the Bible appear to differ, the pious Christian immediately concludes that he has not understood the Bible', he wrote. One imagines that if this point of view had prevailed in the Church of England, there would have been very much less controversy over homosexuality in recent years.

Jowett made the case for reading the Bible as 'any other book'. This meant accepting that St Paul and Apostles were products of their time and had no access to abstract notions of Christian truth that subsequently developed.

For me the most interesting essay in the collection was from the Oxford Professor of Geometry, Baden Powell.[4] Entitled *The Study of Evidence in Christianity*, it made the point that the life of Jesus cannot both be treated as historical fact and yet be exempt from the processes by which historical facts are established. By extension he felt that Jesus' miracles could not be treated as evidence of his divinity (that should be ascribed to his teachings). While he accepted that the essential doctrines of Christianity were the same 'yesterday, today and forever', he did not believe that the so called 'evidences of revelation' were equally eternal. 'These external accessories constitute a subject which of necessity is perpetually taking somewhat at least of a new form with the successive phases of opinion and knowledge',[5] he wrote. He also doubted the historicity of miracles: 'Difficulties in the idea of suspensions of natural laws in former ages were not at all canvassed or thought of, but in later times they have assumed a much deeper importance'.[6] He went as far as to suggest that it might be blasphemous to believe that the miracles happened as reported, as such a belief would undermine God's natural laws.

One suspects that if Powell were alive today, Richard Dawkins and other scientific rationalists would have found little grounds for disagreement. Christianity might still be seen as the ally of free thinking and innovation in academia rather than its natural enemy.

Unfortunately, Powell died of a heart attack before the second big event of 1860. This was a meeting of the British Academy for the Advancement of Science on 30 June, to celebrate the opening of Oxford's Museum of Natural History. It is today remembered as the Great Evolution Debate. It saw Bishop Wilberforce confront the eminent biologist, Thomas Henry Huxley, over Charles Darwin's theory of evolution. It was not a meeting of minds. Wilberforce is said[7] to asked whether Huxley would prefer to 'be descended from an ape on his mother's side or his father's?' To which Huxley replied that he would 'sooner claim kindred with an ape than with a man like the bishop who made so ill a use of his wonderful speaking powers'.

The confrontation is often described as the moment that science and Christianity parted company. This interpretation only became common 30 or 40 years after the event.[8] At the time there were churchmen and scientists on both sides. For example, Temple gave a sermon in the University Church the day after the debate making the case for Darwin, while the eminent physicist, Sir David Brewster, who was the principal of Edinburgh University supported Wilberforce (in fact Brewster's wife fainted as the debate reached its crescendo).

Powell had been scheduled to speak in the debate in favour of Darwin. He was an enthusiastic supporter. In his contribution to *Essays and Reviews*, he described *The Origin of the Species* as a 'masterly volume' which 'must soon bring about an entire revolution of opinion in favour of the grand principle of the self-evolving powers of nature'.[9] He described creation as 'only another name for our ignorance of the mode of production'. Darwin himself appreciated Powell's support of *The Origin of the Species*, remarking that the Professor of Geometry had 'converted many readers and induced them to give up the doctrine of creation'.[10]

Powell was also a Church of England priest. Huxley, by contrast, was an agnostic.[11] If Powell had survived long enough to lead the defence of Darwin, things might have turned out very differently. Perhaps the divide between science and religion might never have opened up. Instead, the divide would be between those religious people who found it possible to accommodate science within their reading of the Bible and those who did not.

The University authorities responded to Darwin's theory of evolution by changing the design of the entrance to the Oxford Natural History Museum. It originally featured the characters of Adam and Eve. This was changed to a carving of an angel holding a Bible in one hand and a cell, representing biological science, in the other. It seemed to be a way of symbolically showing that the University represented progress while remaining true to its motto: the Lord is my light.

The response of the University Church to the events of 1860 was to appoint John William Burgon as its incumbent. His picture remains today in the church vestry with the caption 'The most orthodox vicar of St Mary's'. It is a reminder that after the furore around *Essays and Reviews*, clergy in the Church of England faced two choices: being orthodox or being quiet. It is a legacy that continues today.

This legacy of silence is another reason I am writing this book. I don't see the clergy doing it. More than 160 years later, what Jowett referred to as 'the abominable system of terrorism', which stops priests from freely speaking their mind about God in public, continues to be in force. It is not that I want more sermons about science. It is that there are questions thrown up by social and environmental change that I want answers to. They are reshaping the way each of us understands our conscience, but the Church struggles to offer leadership. Who in church is having an honest conversation about faith and diversity? It is a knotty issue when there are White churches and Black churches; religions segmented by geography; and uncompromising beliefs in universal truth. Similarly, how do you paint the Gospels green when the very concept of environmental degradation did not exist in Jesus' day? What is the meaning of personal salvation when the planet itself is going to hell?

Temple suggested that when conscience and the Bible appeared to differ, the pious Christian should reinterpret the Bible. I think it has gone beyond that. When conscience doesn't find easy answers in the Bible, the pious Christian should look elsewhere for inspiration. That is how atheist books become gospels.

The Big Ideas

My objective in setting up the youth discussion group at the University Church was to make sure that those who came to it (including me) were building their faith upon a rock. Doing that means being able to confront all the big ideas of atheism. What I soon discovered was that atheist authors are much more interesting from a religious perspective than Christian ones. Christian writers can be inspirational, but they tend not to be challenging. Atheist books on the other hand go straight to the weak points in the argument for God. They force you to think. The extraordinary thing is that the more you think about them the more inspirational those books become. That is because their authors are thinking around areas where one might say angels fear to tread. Some of what they say is true. Some of it is contentious. By looking for what is true and contending what is contentious one can expand one's understanding of God.

In the next four chapters I am going to look at big ideas that have grown out of four books written by atheist authors since 1860. They represent the four ideas that I think are most challenging to conventional religious thinking to emerge during that time. Each of them, for me, helps answer a specific question about the nature of God which one won't find in conventional religious literature.

I will introduce each of the four books below, giving a short explanation of what we can expect to get out of them.

Thus Spoke Zarathustra by Friedrich Nietzsche
(published between 1883–1885)

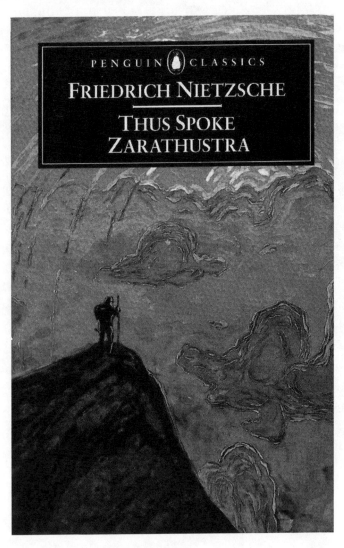

This reads like a missing book of the Old Testament set in Tolkien's Middle Earth, rewritten by an acid-addled rock star. It follows Zarathustra in his travels and preaching as he tries to explain the meaning of the death of God. The basic idea is that without God we need to find within ourselves an alternative to nihilism in order to motivate our lives. That something is our 'will to power' which we must use to create our own greatness.

No German philosopher with a cluster of five consonants in the middle of his name is ever going to be mainstream, but Nietzsche's thinking has permeated society without being widely read. This has happened because his self-centred, subjective view of the world, seems to mirror the default way in which humans view themselves when they don't feel the need to think about God.

Christians often assume that because someone doesn't believe in God, they can't be a moral person or have a real purpose in life. Nietzsche says that they can. They can create their own morality after throwing off the vestiges of Christian thinking. They can also define their own purpose; they can become the greatest version of themselves. This self-overcoming is the true objective of life, Nietzsche argues.

In the chapter on *Thus Spoke Zarathustra* I will aim to answer the question: is religion good? That seems to be the first question anyone approaching belief should have. Why join a religion if doing so increases suffering in the world? Nietzsche thought that the death of God represented the liberation of mankind from a destructive kind of slavery. At the same time, he showed an ambivalence towards the person of Jesus that invites a deeper exploration of where the fault lies. Is it with God or the way that we pursue religion?

Writing and Difference by **Jacques Derrida**
(published 1967)

This is the most obscure book on the reading list. It is a collection of essays and lectures translated from French that can't have been read cover to cover by more than 10,000 people. Yet it is probably the most influential in terms of the way it has reshaped the way the western world thinks. It did this in two ways. First it provided the tools to challenge the hierarchies of race, gender, and class that were embedded in western literature and culture. These tools have since become the weapons with which the war over identity politics is fought. Secondly, it promulgated the idea that there is no definitive meaning of a text. Rather, there are an infinite number of possible readings — some of which might be completely opposed to the author's original intent — each with an equal value. This idea could be said to provide the basis for post-truth politics; everything and nothing can be claimed as truth. This has obvious implications for reading the Bible.

To many readers these ideas might epitomise the very worst kind of left-wing pseudo-intellectualism. Nevertheless, they are difficult to dismiss. Unless we can insert ourselves inside the author's head at the very moment they write a sentence, we can never perfectly capture what that sentence might mean. The connections and associations we make are always going to be a function of our time and perspective. Furthermore, all writing does contain hidden assumptions that reveal the prejudices of that time and perspective. As society becomes more fractious these are bound to be challenged by those who feel silenced or disadvantaged by them. Derrida's writing goes to the heart of the paradox: we need a common intellectual framework to understand a world in which there can be no common intellectual framework.

In the chapter on *Writing and Difference* I will aim to answer the question: how do we know God? We rely on ancient texts, but what if we are forced to accept that their meaning is fluid and indefinite? Derrida argues that this makes God impossible. But does it? Could it in fact say something quite profound about the nature of God and our relationship with Him or Her?

A Brief History of Time by Stephen Hawking
(published 1988)

This is the bestselling book in the line-up. It has sold more than 25 million copies since publication, reflecting the huge interest in the origins of the universe and the attraction of a layman's guide to it. Despite ending with the promise that we might one day be able to know 'the mind of God', the book is profoundly atheist in intent. Hawking's objective is to explain how the universe might have come into being without the need for a creator or an 'unmoved mover'.

I will use the chapter on this book to answer the question: where is God? Hawking's answer is nowhere. There is no time or space for Him or Her to exist before the beginning of time. Many Christians prefer to separate science entirely from religion to imagine a wholly immaterial God. This God occupies a land of purpose and meaning without trespassing on physics or physical reality. I think that it could all be a lot simpler than that. Hawking's book inadvertently provides us with the answer.

The God Delusion by **Richard Dawkins**
(published 2006)

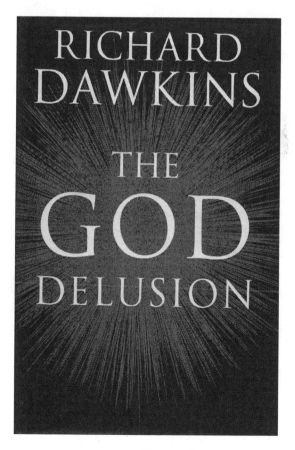

This is the only 'gospel' I write about in this book which was explicitly written to stop people believing in God. Its central thesis is that religion is dangerous nonsense. It is dangerous because of the litany of abuses and suffering that can be laid at the door of religion. It is nonsense because it has no rational basis. Furthermore, the danger and the nonsense are connected according to Dawkins. It is because religion does not listen to reason that it is such a menace to the world. Nothing, apart from a refusal to believe, can stop it, he argues.

In Church sermons today, Dawkins is often referenced as a pantomime villain. A preacher will mention his name as someone who is obviously wrong and probably going to hell for it. There is very little effort to engage with his arguments. I think that is a mistake. If what Dawkins says about religion is true — and much of it is — then religions are clearly failing to live up to their own objectives. We must do better.

Dawkins talks about 'blind faith' as the biggest danger to the world. That seems to be a mistake. It seems to me that faith is the opposite; it is a way of seeing. I will use *The God Delusion* to answer the question: what is faith?

How This Book Works

There will be some readers who might already be quailing at the thought of wading through an intellectual analysis of four scholarly tomes. It isn't as scary as it seems. As I said earlier, the book grew out of a teenage church discussion group. My job was to make the ideas in each book we discussed accessible to an 11-year-old. The experience of digesting these books confirmed a prejudice I have long held: if an idea can't be explained to an 11-year-old, it probably isn't much of an idea. All the ideas I talk about in this book are bold and simple.

Each chapter is divided into four sections: an introduction to the book in question; a bit of background on the author; an outline of the big ideas in the book and a dialogue recreating how I discussed the ideas with the University Church discussion group; and a conclusion.

The dialogue is mostly based on my memory of how things went, but there are a number of complications. The young people who took part — particularly my own children — wouldn't thank me if they were readily identifiable in the book. The cast of characters also changed a lot over the decade that I ran the group, so there has been some merging of the people. Furthermore, in real life the discussions often went extravagantly off topic. I let it happen because it helped create an atmosphere in which the young people felt they could say what they liked. From the point of view of this book, the dialogues are important as they help emphasise the broader point that Christianity should be seen as an act of exploration in a world of flux rather than a fixed destination.

For ease of reference the dramatis personae are:

Rosamond is in her A-Level year studying sciences. She is quite thoughtful but not wholly expansive about what she believes.

George is in his A-Level year and is very well read on theological topics. He has a broad intellectual grasp of all of the issues and comes across as a bit earnest.

Harry, George's younger brother is 16 and sees himself as a confirmed atheist. He comes to the discussion group because he enjoys the intellectual engagement — and keeping his brother on his toes.

Marion is an easy-going girl in the lower sixth form. She doesn't seem to have any significant doubts about Christianity, but she does have a good sense of when things sound hollow.

Freya is Marion's sister and the youngest member of the group, aged just 11. She is very bright but has something of a butterfly mind, which makes it difficult to know whether to take her seriously or not.

Rowan is 12 and joined us having previously attended a more conservative evangelical Church. He is a little unsure of what to make of our religious free-for-all, and is relatively quiet.

James is 13 and takes a sceptical view of religion but is interested in hearing what we have to say, as long as no one puts him on the spot about his beliefs. Despite this reticence he is usually quick to spot the weakness of an argument.

As for me, I am not a clergyman. I am a layman whose day job is in financial journalism. That gives me a freedom to say things that most of the clergy don't have. I can say things about Christianity which are probably obvious to most people in the pews, but which are still difficult for priests to articulate, for fear of offending the defenders of the orthodoxy. I have written this book for the following groups of people:

Atheists who want to consider the possibility of belief. Many of you know all the reasons why you should not believe in God, and are completely unconvinced by the conventional arguments for faith. You are also likely to be suspicious of conventional religion, but still feel a sense of incompleteness which you assume might once have been filled by religion. I want you to read this book and feel that you can become a secret Christian, enriching your life in the pursuit of the gospel of love without compromising your values.

Liberal Christians who feel that they are not getting many answers from the pulpit. It is one of the great frustrations of the church that the clergy are often so timid in the way they think in public. I hope this book will inspire you (and them) to believe boldly.

Catholics whose faith is wearing thin. I have attended Catholic churches in the past, and I very much enjoy the Catholic intellectual tradition in literature. My impression of the Faith is that it is like a richly woven tapestry. Its doctrine is all fine and intricately designed on the side that faces the world, but quite knotted on the reverse; the side which faces your mind. This book is quite antithetical to Catholic doctrine; but I hope, if you feel you have reached a bald patch in the tapestry, it will help provide some reinforcement to the knotting on the reverse.

Conservative evangelicals who want to see Christianity in a different way. The evangelical tradition is often presented to its members as an all-or-nothing proposition. It means that, particularly for young people growing up in an evangelical Church, small questions about one thing can often lead to the rejection of the whole. I hope that this book will help you to find a way to stay with Christianity and explore its paradoxes and subtleties.

Most of all this book is written for those who are excited by the possibilities of God in a post-modern, scientific world of many faiths and none. Everything I know about God suggests that He or She delights in the creative possibilities of the future.

Chapter 2

Friedrich Nietzsche: *Thus Spoke Zarathustra*

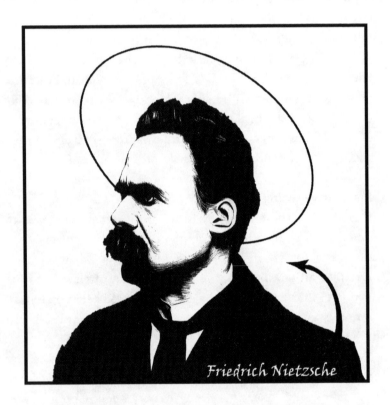

Friedrich Nietzsche

Is Religion Good?

Introduction

Zarathustra announces in the prologue of Nietzsche's book that 'God is Dead'.[12] We are not going to find him alive again in this chapter. What we are going to find is the shape that God leaves when He or She is taken out of the picture.

But we will find out more about God in this chapter than just this negative shape. Despite being an atheist, Nietzsche was also a believer. He believed that life should have purpose.

Nihilism — the idea that life is pointless or without meaning — is as much his enemy as God. This makes him much more interesting as an atheist writer than others who get rid of God and leave us nothing to live for in God's stead.

Exploring this belief in purpose is a good place to start this book. Unless you have had a mystical religious experience or you have been brought up to be convinced of the truth of a particular religion, this is where everyone's journey to God starts: a yearning for purpose. And where better to start than *Thus Spoke Zarathustra*? The book is Christianity's ground zero. God is dead; all we have around us are the ruins of a derelict religion, and even these must be torn down. Amidst the rubble and debris, however, we find this single sprig of thought: that there is purpose. Let's read on to find out what it will it grow into.

Where Is Nietzsche Coming From?

From the future. That is the short answer. Nietzsche's writing was not much noticed by his contemporaries. *Thus Spoke Zarathustra* was published in four parts during the early 1880s, but sales of the first three parts were miserable and he had to print the final instalment in an edition of 40 copies at his own expense. He struggled even to give away those copies. Yet today Nietzsche's thinking seems to permeate our society in the most extraordinary way. Furthermore, it seems more relevant now than it was 10 years ago, and more relevant 10 years ago than it was 100 years before that.

This probably sounds like an exaggeration. Most people probably haven't heard of Nietzsche and very few have read his books. So why do I say that he is so influential? Influential is probably the wrong word. Prophetic would be a better one. We should understand him as the first prophet of atheism. There were plenty of atheist writers before Nietzsche, but their philosophies were largely insipid. They avoided direct confrontation with a religious world view. Instead they tended to suggest that the best we can do is accept life as it is. The oldest ones are:

- Epicureanism: 'Eat, drink, and be merry for tomorrow we may die'.
- Stoicism: 'Grant me the serenity to accept the things I cannot change, courage to change the things I can, and wisdom to know the difference'.[13]
- Cynicism: 'Life is a bad joke. You've got to laugh'.

None of them directly deny the existence of God. Nietzsche does. He writes like a conquistador just landed on the continent of a dying God: he is determined not to rest until the last vestiges of religion have been rooted out, and he has planted his own ideas in their place.

The premise of *Thus Spoke Zarathustra* is the question: 'what should we believe in if we can no longer believe in God?' His answer stretches to 328 pages in the Penguin translation, but it boils down to one thing: the transformative power of ourselves. This is more than just an answer. It is a perspective.

Most philosophers approach truth as if life were a field sport; a game where the same rules must apply to all the players, otherwise it won't work. Nietzsche doesn't see it that way. He sees life as a first-person shooter video game. The only player who is actually real is the one at the controls. 'In the final analysis, one only experiences oneself', Zarathustra remarks at the beginning of Part 3 of the book.[14]

This perspective grows immediately out of Nietzsche's atheism. If there is no all-seeing God watching over everything to act as referee, does anyone else's view of the world matter? If not, what does matter? His answer is that we matter. The purpose of life is to become the greatest version of ourselves, creating our own values rather than accepting those of others.

Thus Spoke Zarathustra does not expound this thesis from A to B in plain terms. Instead, it approaches the subject sideways in a format reminiscent of holy scripture, complete with sermons, psalms, goats, honey and prophetic hairdos. It is the most crazy and confounding book to read. It has a sort of plot. Zarathustra leaves the mountains to impart his message about the death of God to the world. He is rejected, picks up some followers, returns to the cave where he lives and eventually there is a moment of apotheosis as he realises his ideal. In between he does a lot of preaching to himself, to his followers and to his animals (a serpent and an eagle who join him when he despairs of winning over the masses). Most of these sermons are delivered as a series of often bombastic aphorisms. As Zarathustra explains: 'Of all writings I love only that which is written with blood. Write with blood and you will discover that blood is spirit... He who writes in blood and aphorisms does not want to be read, he wants to be learned by heart'.[15]

This idea of writing in blood for the heart is also part of Nietzsche's unique perspective. For him, philosophy is not just an intellectual pursuit for academic seminars. It is lived with one's entire being. He saw in the human psyche a side that was primeval, chaotic and irrational (the Dionysian he called it). This he felt was as much part of us as our reasoned intellect.

This view provides a difficult challenge for those who believe in a grand sweep of history moving from darkness to light; from the ignorance and superstition of religion to enlightenment, reason, and universal values. Rather, it suggests that as we shake off religion, identity, self-expression and the fragmentation of common values should follow. Looking at social trends today, Nietzsche's view of a world without God seems more prescient than a belief in that over the long term the passage of time takes us to a better world. We do live our lives increasingly as if we are controlling an avatar in a computer game rather than playing a team sport. Facebook, Instagram and

TikTok have reinforced this sense. Main character syndrome — where everyone else is just the supporting cast in our personal story — has become a common trope. In politics, the concept of universal values is steadily receding. Both the left and the right question the inherent bias of any system that attempts to give equal rights to all. Instead, politics is fought over questions of identity. We have moved from a world where there was a single generally agreed version of the truth to one in which what you believe to be true is likely to be a function of who you are.

The crazy thing is that the Church itself is right at the front line of this culture war. It has not risen above narcissistic individualism and identity politics or proved itself to be the last bastion of universal values. Instead, its disparate branches find themselves in the trenches fighting alongside extremes of the right and left. It would seem to confirm the death of God. In the absence of divine authority, the Church is just another group of factions vying for power in a post-religious world.

This book would end here if that were all there was to say about *Thus Spoke Zarathustra*. Fortunately, there is more. There is more to Nietzsche than his bold atheism. His greatest gift is his insight into the human condition. That is where we can begin to find God among the ruins of twenty-first-century religion.

Nietzsche and Nazism

All this might make it seem as if Nietzsche was a political philosopher. In fact, he was the very reverse. He despised the state. According to Zarathustra 'whatever the State says, it lies; whatever the state has, it has stolen. Everything about it is false: it bites with stolen teeth'.[16] He equally hated popular opinion. His books are unashamedly addressed to the elite few who have the mind to understand him. Furthermore, he really didn't like the concept of followers. He wanted everyone to follow their own ideas rather than behave like sheep. That said, if you take the view that the very concept of universal values is an obsolete vestige of a Christian past, you should not be surprised if anti-democratic and illiberal people find inspiration in your writing. Especially if you say things like: 'You should love peace as a means to new wars, and the short peace more than the long'.[17] Or, 'Live your life of obedience and war! What good is long life? What warrior wants to be spared?'[18]

Of course, he meant these things to be interpreted metaphorically. He is commending his readers to wage war for their opinions, but he wasn't around to control how his books were read. In 1889 he had a nervous breakdown and was incoherent for the rest of his life until he died in 1900. His sister, a profound antisemite, took responsibility for his literary legacy. Together with her husband she had left Germany in 1887 to set up in Paraguay a pure Aryan community named Nueva Germania. When it failed, she returned to Germany to care for her brother, editing his works to reflect her own ideology. After the First World War she became closely associated with the Nazi movement, to the extent that when she died in 1935, Hitler attended her funeral.

Nietzsche himself despised nationalism and antisemitism. 'Deutschland, Deutschland über alles, I am afraid that was the end of German philosophy',[19] he wrote, and 'I will have all antisemites shot'.[20] Despite his apparent glorification of warriors, he was a miserable soldier himself. During the Franco Prussian war he served as a medical orderly, contracting diphtheria, dysentery and possibly syphilis.

Nietzsche's martial metaphors were just that. Metaphors. When Zarathustra speaks of war and warriors he is quite clear about what he means. 'You should seek your enemy, you should wage your war — a war for your opinion.'[21] The reason Nietzsche praises martial values and writes like a conquistador is because he thinks it is important for each of us to stand up and fight for who we are. It is what makes him a great writer, but it doesn't protect him from the worst readers. These, he said, 'are those who behave like plundering troops: they take away a few things they can use, dirty and confound the remainder, and revile the whole'.[22] I will try not to behave like that in what follows.

What Is the Big Idea?

Nietzsche has many. Let's look at them one by one.

1) God Is Dead

Unlike some of the other writers covered in this book, Nietzsche doesn't see the need to explain his atheism. He takes it as a matter of fact, or as he says in his earlier book, *The Gay Science*: 'belief in God has become unbelievable'. He doesn't say this because an understanding of science casts a shadow over his belief. He didn't have much respect for scientists: 'How much boundlessly stupid naivety is there in the scholar's belief in his superiority, in the simple, unsuspecting certainty with which his instincts treat the religious man as inferior and a lower type which he himself has evolved above and beyond', he wrote. It was a much more personal revelation. One so intense that if it turned out that God were not dead, Nietzsche would almost certainly kill Him.[23]

Hating something with a passion like this inevitably has a back story. Nietzsche's father and both grandfathers were Lutheran pastors. He grew up a pious child and initially he intended to follow in their footsteps. At the age of 18 he wrote a poem expressing his devotion to Christ. It includes the verse:

'I am filled with horror at the dark power of sin,
And I cannot look back.
I must not lose thee,
At night, terrified and oppressed, I see thee,
I see thee and I cannot let thee go.'[24]

It sounds incredibly committed. The sort of thing someone who calls themselves a 'strong' Christian might write today. But it was not what it seemed. This youth, who was lying awake at night tortured by the consequences of sin, was at the same time intensely worried that the whole of religion might be a fraud. In an essay entitled *Fate and History*, written in the same year that he wrote the above poem, he expressed these doubts: 'There will be great revolutions once the masses finally realize that the totality of Christianity is grounded in presuppositions; the existence of God, immortality, Biblical authority, inspiration, and other doctrines will always remain problems'.[25]

At that stage it seems that the only thing that stood in the way of declaring himself an atheist was the enormity of such a move. He could not break from the culture that had nurtured him.

'The power of habit, the need to strive for higher ideals, the break with all that is established, the dissolution of all forms of society, the question whether mankind hasn't been deceived for two thousand years by a phantom, the sense of one's arrogance and rashness: all struggle against one another in an uncertain strife until, finally, painful experiences and mournful events lead our heart back again to the old childhood beliefs.'[26]

Three years later, in 1865, when he was a 20-year-old student studying theology and philosophy at Bonn University, he did finally develop the confidence to break with Christianity. What seems to have sowed the seeds of doubt was the feeling that everything he believed about God sprang mainly from the accident of his birth. He wrote to his sister, Elizabeth, at the time of his decision to abandon the study of theology as follows:

'If we have believed from childhood that all salvation issued from someone other than Jesus — say, from Mohammed — is it not certain that we should have experienced the same blessings?'[27]

This reasoning is probably the biggest reason why faith is no longer passed down the generations as it was, say, 100 years ago. I have heard it in our youth discussion group at St Mary's many times. Those who take part are acutely aware that they live in a multicultural, multifaith world. They don't want to be part of a Church that condemns other people's beliefs as misguided, and they don't want to accept a hand-me-down from their family in an unthinking way. If they are open to belief in God, they feel that they ought to choose a religion in the same way that they might choose a university course; reading the prospectuses and perhaps visiting the different campuses. Quickly, however, they realise that this is not how it works. They recognise that they would struggle to accept the tenets of Islam or Hinduism without having been brought up in a family and a culture that might condition them to accept those beliefs. Some leave it there and conclude that Christianity is the benign idiocy of an older generation. Others take it further. They begin to see something quite dark in the idea of religion. They ask themselves: 'If God is a product of culture and we are told to accept that there is just one true God, does that mean that other cultures which follow other religions are wrong? If so, how is that different from racism?' Sitting in the University Church we are surrounded by memorials of empire: a statue of Cecil Rhodes peers in the windows from across the High Street; a well-polished brass on the wall commemorates the Oxfordshire soldiers killed in Baluchistan in the 1880s; a stone monument remembers a magistrate working for the East India Company in Calcutta. In these circumstances it is difficult to miss the potential for religion to become an instrument of power and oppression.

This is how Nietzsche sees religion. It is not a benign response to the pain and suffering in the world which offers salvation in a different world. It is the actual cause of that pain and suffering, and it must be defeated in this world and every trace of its thinking erased.[28]

This last point is probably the most important part of Zarathustra's message. From Nietzsche's point of view, when God is dead, what is the point of morality? Isn't it also an instrument of oppression, a code of conduct imposed on us and designed to hold us back? Zarathustra preaches that we should free ourselves from this burden, create our own values and become who we were meant to be. Morality, as a vestige of religion is also part of the problem rather than part of the solution to the struggles of life.

Sidebar: Weaponizing Morality

Can we really dispose of morality so easily? The belief that it is good to be good seems so deeply ingrained in us that it almost seems to be us. What are we but our values?

One of the most intriguing books that our youth discussion group at the University Church took on was Chris Paley's *Beyond Bad*.[29] It knocks the concept of morality off its pedestal. Our sense of right and wrong evolved simply because humans needed to work in groups in order to be effective. Morality, he argues, is really just 'groupish-ness': a way of saying who is in and who is out, so we can work more effectively with each other.

His reasoning is that as individuals, the human species is not really that good at anything. We are not particularly strong or fast and we don't have big teeth or claws. Working in groups, however, we can become masters of the environment. Early man could kill mammoths and sabre-toothed tigers, cultivate land, nurture and protect the young. But working in groups is not easy if everyone is pursuing their own selfish instinct. Why risk your life fighting a sabre-toothed tiger when you can hang back at the campfire feasting on mammoth steaks? There has to be a way of ensuring that everyone is committed to contributing to the success of the group regardless of their selfish instincts. It is what we call morality. Moral groups outperform amoral groups because they can work more cohesively to achieve their ends. 'Humans are the only species that have stumbled upon a way to properly manage the conflicts of interests and cooperate within groups that aren't genetically related', Paley argues.[30]

Where the book gets interesting is when he starts to unpick how morality works. The objective is to promote group values by rewarding conformity and punishing transgression, but there is a lot of subtlety in the way that we do this. For example, you don't need to be too good. You just need to behave in a way that is within the bounds of the group's expectations. He cites studies that show that if people are first given the opportunity to publicly signal that they are virtuous, they are subsequently much more likely to make a less virtuous choice when they think it is being made in private.

Actual virtue usually comes at a price because it typically involves some self-sacrifice. So people are always on the lookout for easy alternatives. The best one is being censorious of other people's behaviour. If you are seen to punish harshly other people who don't conform to the group's behaviour, then people will think you really care about the group's values. You don't actually have to be good to be thought of as good.

In the past, morality had a higher cost that it does today. Burning wrong-doers in boiling oil or going out on a crusade was troublesome and expensive. Today we can burnish our reputations for being good group members on social media at the touch of a hashtag. It makes Paley's theory immediately relatable to the young people in our discussion group.

In the book, Paley doesn't labour the connection between morality and religion, but the implications are clear. Religions evolved as the arbiters of morality, enforcing its strictures through low-cost threats and rewards in the afterlife. (In this reading, social media might in fact turn out to be the biggest threat to religion because it polices group values without the need for paying salaries to priests.)

Besides talking about the mechanics of morality, Paley also makes the fascinating suggestion that morals have shaped the evolution of the human mind. If we know that we will be judged as much by our intentions as we are by the outcome of our actions, then it becomes important to be able to think about how other people think we are thinking. This, Paley suggests, may have provided the impetus for the development of consciousness: 'Without morals you wouldn't even have a mind', he argues.[31]

Despite this, Paley believes, like Nietzsche, that morality is obsolete. It stands in the way of our future both as individuals and as a species. It exists as much to divide people as it exists to unite them. It makes practical solutions to conflicts of interest more difficult to resolve. His book concludes with the words: 'Our collective actions will, most likely, destroy the globe. It is morality that got us here. We needed in our infancy [...] But we're grown-ups now. It is time we left home.'[32]

2) The Will to Power

So there is no God. What does that leave us with? 'Ourselves' is the best answer that Nietzsche can offer. And what are we? At the core of our nature is our 'will to power'. This is what drives life. Zarathustra explains it: 'Where I found a living creature, there I found will to power; and even in the will of the servant I found the will to be master'.[33]

He seems to be right here. We are familiar with the idea of the will to live. It seems to be a precondition of our survival. However, Nietzsche develops the idea further. If we want to live, we must want to flourish and grow to become a greater version of ourselves. We must also want to shape the world so that we can make the most of it. For Nietzsche, the will to power is the overriding purpose of life. He argues that we must recognise it within us and live accordingly.

That means throwing off the restrictions we might impose on our behaviour because we want to be thought of as good. Great people don't live by other people's values. They live by their own values, and the rest of the world accommodates them. In a later book, *On the Genealogy of Morality*, Nietzsche develops this idea. He argues that in the heroic age, the values of society were determined by the strong-willed and this 'master morality' was imposed on everyone else. This morality treasured nobility and power without any thought for the weak. Then the weak took over, and hating the oppression of the strong, they invented a slave morality that ensnared the strong. It valued equality and the good of the community over expressions of great wills. Christianity is a slave morality. If we are to express our will to power, we must escape it.

At this point Nietzsche begins to sound obnoxious, but at the same time there is a tantalising possibility that he might be right. We have all been brought up to believe that it is good to be good. It seems fundamental to our being. Equality and the good of the community are also important to us. The reason humanity has evolved away from the so-called heroic age is because it didn't deliver the greatest happiness to the greatest number. At the same time, we know that when we tell someone to be good, we are also telling them to be submissive, to fit in, to deny themselves. If we only live this one life, why should we allow ourselves to be held back by this? Especially when we look around and see that great people — great artists, billionaires, powerful leaders — don't live by the same morality as the rest of us.

Is Nietzsche waking us up from a benign slumber to tell us the harsh truth about morality? It is a proposition straight out of the movie *The Matrix*.[34] Do we take the Blue Pill and carry on believing the benign fantasy that religion and morality exist essentially to make the world a better place? Or do we take the Red Pill and learn the 'truth': that the concept of goodness only exists to oppress humanity? Let's take the Red Pill and see where Nietzsche's argument takes us.

Sidebar: There Is No Life of Pi

Nietzsche's big fear when he wrote *Thus Spoke Zarathustra* was that in the absence of God, society would fall to nihilism: the belief that life is ultimately random, pointless and empty. Today this still seems the most logical alternative having dismissed God. However, even the most ardent atheist often finds it difficult to look nihilism in the face. It is so dismal to consider that we only think about it in the darkest corners of life. The way we recoil so instinctively from contemplating the possibility of emptiness raises a difficult question: are all our wonderings about meaning and purpose in life just a way of avoiding the unutterable truth that there really is nothing?

One book which takes up this issue is Yann Martel's *Life of Pi*. It has been turned into an award-winning movie and a successful play. It tells the story of a boy (Pi) from Pondicherry in India who starts to follow all three major world religions — Hinduism, Christianity and Islam — before his zoo-owning family take the decision to emigrate, taking the animals with them by boat to Canada. The ship sinks during a storm and Pi finds himself marooned on a lifeboat with an injured zebra, an orangutang, and a hyena. The hyena kills and eats the zebra, and then kills the orangutang, much to the distress of the boy. The zoo's tiger then reveals himself on the lifeboat and kills the hyena. Pi is then left alone on the lifeboat with the tiger (whom he learns to control) for six months before he is washed ashore in Mexico. The tiger lopes away, never to be seen again, but Pi is taken to hospital where he recounts his story to two Japanese shipping inspectors who want to understand what happened to the boat. They find Pi's story unbelievable, so he offers an alternative. In this one there are no animals. Only Pi, his mother, an injured sailor, and a brutal cook make it to the lifeboat. The cook kills the sailor and then Pi's mother but is then himself killed by Pi. The shipping inspectors see that the animals are allegories of the people on the lifeboat. They identify Pi himself as the tiger. Seeing that the shipping inspectors don't believe his first explanation, Pi asks which story they would *rather* believe. They prefer the one with the animals.

The book is billed as 'a story that will make you believe in God'. The implication is that religion is a story that we tell ourselves to come to terms with the fact that life, in its unvarnished state, is too grim to face.

The young people in our University Church discussion group were not convinced. 'If it doesn't matter what you believe, why not just be a Jedi?', one of them remarked. There was a strong feeling that religions should somewhere be grounded in truth. Nietzsche would have agreed. In the same letter to his sister written in 1865, quoted above, when he gave up his theological studies, he wrote: 'Faith does not offer the least support for a proof of objective truth. Here the ways of men part: if you wish to strive for peace of soul and pleasure, then believe; if you wish to be a devotee of truth, then inquire'.

3) Self-Overcoming
The slave morality of Christianity has made the whole of society undistinguished, Nietzsche believes. 'No herdsman and one herd. Everyone wants the same, everyone is the same: whoever thinks otherwise goes voluntarily into the madhouse',[35] Zarathustra explains. In order to escape this fate, those who live boldly must learn to overcome themselves.

The objective of this self-overcoming is the Superman. 'Man is a rope, fastened between animal and Superman — a rope over an abyss,' he says.[36] The abyss is the nihilism that Nietzsche felt was so dangerous to humanity. The Superman is our hope of transcendence; the possibility of experiencing life beyond the normal level. As Nietzsche sees it, there are three stages to this transformation. First, we become like a camel: that is to say, a beast who likes to bear loads. In this stage we actually want to be weighed down by the commandments and strictures of religion and society. We think that carrying these loads is the greatest objective in life.

The second stage arrives when the camel wants freedom. It wants be lord in its own desert. It questions why it should submit to bearing loads? This brings about a confrontation with the camel's ultimate God. In Zarathustra's telling, this God is a dragon with golden scales. Every scale glitters with a commandment: 'Thou Shalt!', representing the values of a thousand years, passed down and imposed on the world.[37]

The dragon says to the camel: 'All values have already been created, and all created values are in me'. The camel cannot respond. Instead it changes to become a lion and roars at the dragon, 'I will!' But it is not enough that the lion should oppose the dragon. It is not a creator of values. Zarathustra explains that in order to become a creator of values it must become a child. 'The child is innocence and forgetfulness, a new beginning, a sport, a self-propelling wheel, a first. Motion, a sacred "Yes".'[38]

This 'yes' brings freedom, levity and an overwhelming love of life. We see the world as it is, without being bound by its cares and its suffering. The Superman, Zarathustra explains, climbs to great heights and 'laughs at all tragedies real and imaginary'.[39]

This might all sound a bit mystical for someone who has taken the Red Pill and is expecting unvarnished reality. Camels, lions, dragons and Supermen all sound a bit fantastical. Wouldn't it be better if Nietzsche told it like a conventional self-help book? He could start with a relatable anecdote showing how he felt liberated by throwing off the expectations of society and how he then created his own values by which to live. He could expound the basic hypothesis that if we experience life through ourselves alone, then our greatest aspiration in life should be to express that self in the way that we live. The next few chapters should be filled with real life examples of people who have lived by this principal: Julius Caesar, Napoleon, Goethe, and even Jesus and the Buddha might all get a case study as people who have come close to the ideal of the Superman. Each had the force of will to reshape the world around them. Later editions of the book might also include a tricky chapter on Hitler. It would underline the point that the Superman is not a political philosophy; it is a personal one. The final chapter of the book would then read much as the final chapter of Zarathustra reads: a picture of the author living a mellow life in the mountains with the sun shining and feeling totally fulfilled. So much so that he could live his whole life all over again and still feel jokey and playful about it.

Writing a didactic self-help book would completely miss the point, however. It would mean that his readers were not using their imaginations to create their own selves. They would be following his instructions to become exactly the kind of sheepish non-entity that he so much despises. The metaphors, the parables, the fantastical imagery and language with which Nietzsche writes are there to create an uncertainty in interpretation which is quite deliberate. If we are left wondering whether he means Jesus or Hitler when he talks about the Superman, then it is not because Nietzsche's message in Zarathustra is ambiguous. Nietzsche's message is clear: we must see our own values in the Superman that we aspire to become. Those values might be closer to Hitler's or Jesus's, but they must be our own. They are what we most love in ourselves and in the world that we create around us.

4) Eternal Recurrence

I mentioned above how *Zarathustra* ends with the prophet feeling ready to live his life all over again with the same sense of levity. In fact, the idea of living the same life over and over again was how *Thus Spoke Zarathustra* began for Nietzsche. He was walking by Lake Sils in Switzerland's Engadine Valley when he reached a large pyramid-shaped rock and the idea came to him. He described the experience in his later work, *Ecce Homo*: 'I now wish to relate the history of Zarathustra. The fundamental idea of the work, the Eternal Recurrence, the highest formula of a Yes-saying to life that can ever be attained, was first conceived in the month of August 1881. I made a note of the idea on a sheet of paper, with the postscript: "Six thousand feet beyond man and time"'.[40]

He wasn't thinking of reincarnation, nor the possibility that he might make different choices if he were to live his life again. As Zarathustra explains: 'I shall return, with this sun, with this earth ... not to a new life or a better life or a similar life: I shall return eternally to this identical and self-same life'.[41] Initially the idea filled Nietzsche with horror. He could not face it for himself,[42] but he realised that if a person could welcome such an idea, then that person would have lived life to its fullest extent. Needless to say, Zarathustra is such a person. He loves the idea of eternity. He sings songs to it. One of them is inscribed on the same pyramid-shaped rock by the edge of Lake Sils in memory of its inspiration. Translated into English, it ends with the words: 'All desire wants eternity — wants deep, deep eternity!'[43]

The concept of eternal return is another challenge for people who want the unvarnished truth from Nietzsche. It reeks of new age hokum. Clearly history does not, and cannot, repeat itself with such precision. It is perfectly possible to have an infinity of time without the need for the same set of circumstances to repeat themselves eternally.

Some philosophers suggest that the best way of looking at eternal recurrence is as a thought experiment. If one can look at one's life truly and say: 'That was so brilliant, I could do it all again', then it is a good test of whether one has fulfilled one's greatest potential in life. Anyone rewriting *Zarathustra* as a didactic self-help book might labour the point a little more. They might suggest that we should review the things we have done that we would not do again and live in future so we can play 'My Way' or 'Non, je ne regrette rien' at our funerals. However, that would be pretty trite, and misses a lot of the richness of Nietzsche's message.

Nietzsche was trying to understand where a world without God left us, and the idea of eternal recurrence is probably the most effective way of banishing religious thought from the world. For example, if the world has no beginning or end, it has no need for a creator. Furthermore, if the same circumstances can be repeated *ad infinitum*, we need not make a God out of progress (as many scientists do). In a religious world, life on Earth is the entrance exam for a future life which might be better or worse according to the grades we achieve in the judgement of God. If God is dead, then we must mark our own papers and fix our own punishments and rewards. Eternal recurrence is how we might do that. But there is more to it than that. The concept of eternal recurrence also offers an intriguing an answer to the question 'why?'

If we repeatedly ask 'why?' to understand the purpose of things in a religious world view, we ultimately get the answer: 'because God'. It ends there. In a scientific, materialist world view the ultimate answer is 'because our genes work like that'. In eternal recurrence Nietzsche sees an alternative. To explain it, one needs to understand Nietzsche's love of music and dance. These things he felt captured the essence of levity in life. They are frivolous, but not necessarily pointless. As Nietzsche remarked: 'The end of a melody is not its goal: but nonetheless, had the melody not reached its end it would not have reached its goal either. A parable'.[44]

We can listen to a good piece of music over and over again. This is how we should live. It is the process of overcoming ourselves which provides the melody in life, not the objective of becoming the Superman.

Where Is God in *Zarathustra*?

I said at the beginning of this chapter that we wouldn't find God in *Zarathustra*. Nietzsche has killed him. Instead, I suggested we would find the shape left when God is taken out of the picture. On the face of it we lose nothing. Nietzsche presents an extraordinarily compelling alternative to religion that speaks directly to our ego. 'You can be great', he whispers. 'Don't let other people hold you back. Become yourself. Live boldly. Create.' By contrast, when scientific materialists such as Richard Dawkins lose God, the world we are left with is drab and uncompelling. A rational explanation of everything is scarcely enough to live for. Nietzsche celebrates the irrational, the Dionysian; the unfathomable heart of humanity that creates great art, that is capable of terrible and inexplicable things, that has great passions and whimsical curiosities. The death of God does not leave a void. Rather it appears to open out a world rich with wonder and opportunity.

It looks a compelling alternative to God and to nihilism, but there is something unsatisfactory about Nietzsche's vision of the Superman. Zarathustra is not a Napoleon or a Steve Jobs who bends the world to his will through force of personality. He is a misanthropic loner who lives like a hermit in a mountain cave. He might sing songs about how much he loves eternity and welcomes the concept of eternal return — but can anyone claim to have embraced life to the full if they have lived most of it alone on a mountainside with a snake and an eagle?

There is another way of reading *Thus Spoke Zarathustra*: as the story of Nietzsche's failure to find an adequate alternative to God and nihilism. Zarathustra can talk excitedly about the possibilities of moral independence in a godless world, but the only way in which he can detach himself from the morality of the herd, is to detach himself from the herd. That is because, whether or not there is a God, morality is the basis on which we bond with our fellow humans. You may be able to invent your own values, but ultimately if you want to live with other people in a productive way you have to share their values (and they have to share yours). By contrast, Zarathustra sees himself as being driven by a unique creative force: the will to power, but how does he express it? Through dissatisfaction with his fellow humans and a yearning to be alone.

In this reading of *Zarathustra*, what we lose when we take God out of the picture are meaningful relations with everyone else.

I think that there is something immensely significant in this conclusion. It is where we begin to find God in Zarathustra. By a roundabout logic it seems to imply that there is something holy about our connection with other people. As the poet John Donne put it:

No man is an island entire of itself; every man is a piece of the continent, a part of the main.

If a clod be washed away by the sea, Europe is the less, as well as if a promontory were, as well as if a manor of thy friend's or of thine own were.

Any man's death diminishes me, because I am involved in mankind. And therefore never send to know for whom the bell tolls; it tolls for thee.[45]

In this section I will explore this tension between our yearning for connection and our will to become the greatest version of ourselves. These centripetal and centrifugal forces seem to be at the heart of our existence. I will discuss them under two separate headings in the format of our discussion of *Zarathustra* in the youth group at the University Church.

Superman and Interconnectedness

After I gave my potted explanation of *Zarathustra* to the group, I kicked off the conversation by asking for examples of people who might meet Nietzsche's idea of the Superman: i.e. people who lived by their own rules. Lots of names were mentioned: Boris Johnson, Donald Trump, Gru from *Despicable Me*, Cersei Lannister. In the end we settle on Francesca Simon's Horrid Henry as our exemplar. He is a great character. Driven by a Dionysian will to power, he is thwarted at every turn by the snivelling morality of his goody-goody brother, Perfect Peter. He doesn't live by society's rules. He sells his brother to Moody Margaret as a slave. He switches the labels on the Christmas presents so he gets the Boom-Boom Basher (an unspecified noisy and violent toy) while his cousin, Stuck-Up Steve, gets a pair of socks. However, he has a strong sense of fairness and he doesn't like it when Perfect Peter makes him look bad in front of Mum and Dad.

Does this mean that he hasn't really escaped everyone else's morality?

'If he had you probably wouldn't want to read the books,' suggests Rosamond, who is in her A-Level year and seems to have an encyclopaedic knowledge of Horrid Henry. 'You sympathise with him.'

Could we imagine a character who didn't want to look good to anyone?

'They wouldn't have any friends,' says Freya, a confident eleven-year-old who has come along with her older sister, Marion.

'No one would make a film about them,' chips in George, one of the older boys. 'It wouldn't make any money.'

Perhaps it is different in real life. Did Hitler need friends? What about Elon Musk? There is agreement that Hitler needed supporters.

'They weren't his friends. He was just using them,' George points out.

'How do you tell the difference?' asks Rosamond. 'It is like Perfect Peter. He always looks good to Mum and Dad, but that is because he is manipulating them, and always making Henry look bad.'

So is there an important difference between looking good to someone and actually being good to them?

'God knows if you are being bad,' Freya suggests.

'But durr Freya, God is dead,' cuts in Marion.

'You'd know it yourself. Henry feels guilty when he does something that is actually bad rather than just naughty,' says Rosamond.

Would guilt bother someone like Hitler or Boris Johnson?

'I think it would depend on how they were doing. To be really good at manipulating other people you have to know how they feel. I think Boris probably hates himself. He knows he is a liar, but when he is winning he forgets all that,' Rosamond continues before George cuts in.

'I think that if you use people, it is just a means to an end, but having really good friendships is an end in itself. Whatever you use people for has to give you something better.'

Like what?

'Like power or money. But those things are also a means to an end. If I have understood what Nietzsche is trying to say, it's that being yourself is the ultimate end. Like Henry wants to be Henry and do Henry things.'

'And Peter wants to be Peter,' continues Rosamond. 'He manipulates mum and dad so he can be himself.'

I want to steer the discussion round to talk about which is more important: having actual friends or being yourself, but Freya has something urgent to say.

'Do you think Henry would be Henry if Peter wasn't there?'

'That's a good point,' says Rosamond. 'What made you think of it?'

'Sometimes I think about me and Marion. She always says I am useless or stupid, and it makes me want to stand up for myself.'

'That's why I do it, Frey. You should thank me,' Marion explains with sisterly superiority.

So if we get our personality in part from those around us, and we have to be good to people so they like us, can anyone become Nietzsche's Superman?

'Nietzsche isn't talking about now,' George reminds us. 'Zarathustra is preaching about the coming of the Superman in the far future.'

But do you think the Superman is ever going to be possible? They are agreed that it is not. We, as individuals, are so mixed up with each other that we can never escape the rest of humanity and even then it would be an unusual person who actually wanted to do that.

So does that mean God isn't dead?

Eight puzzled faces look my way. Well, if Nietzsche is wrong about the Superman, then is he also wrong about God? They still don't follow, so I explain.

We seem to have come across this idea that we are not each of us individuals on our own. We are also part of the people around us, and they are part of the people around them and we end up all being part of everyone else. What is that thing, that organism that we are all part of? Could we call it God?

None of them are convinced.

Let me put it another way. Do you think we should just be nice to other people so that they are nice to us, or do you think we should be nice to them anyway?

'We should be nice to them anyway,' says Freya.

George's younger brother Harry joins the discussion now. I think he is pretty much confirmed as an atheist, but he comes along to the University Church with his brother for the discussion group on the unspoken condition that I don't question him about his beliefs.

'Obviously we say that we should be nice anyway because it makes us look extra nice. But it isn't true. It is just virtue signalling.'

'Harry, is that what you really think?' George asks.

Harry doesn't like being put on the spot. He replies: 'So what do you think it is? Let's see if you can answer without showing off how virtuous you are.'

'I think you are right that altruism can be seen in purely selfish terms,' Harry begins. 'At the same time virtually no one behaves like that. What about that lady who lives down our road who was arrested for gluing herself to the motorway (in a protest against the lack of action against climate change). Anyone driving around the M25 that day must have really hated her and she had to pay a fine, but she still thought it was the right thing to do. She must be over 70 so she won't benefit from it herself. She is doing it for millions of people who will never know her. Her husband goes to church but she doesn't, so she isn't doing it for religious reasons. How do you explain that?'

'It's virtue signalling as I said,' replies Harry.

'There has to be more to it than that. She is 70 years old. She can't be doing it for likes on Instagram.'

Rosamond then joins in. 'Isn't this what Nietzsche was talking about though: people carrying on as if God was there when they no longer believe in him?'

Yes, I say, but equally it could be that the reason why people continue to behave in a religious way even after they stop believing is because there is this sense that we are all connected. I quote John Donne *For Whom the Bell Tolls*.

They seem to be beginning to grasp my point, but Harry is not convinced.

'So why don't they do it?' he asks.

Do what?

'You say people invented religion because they felt that they were all one big happy family in God or whatever, but it doesn't work like that does it? Religions talk about love and peace and harmony, but they don't do it. Look around you. What they do is hate and kill and fight. It is a joke.'

There is a difficult silence in the room. It is time to bring Nietzsche back into the discussion.

Religion and the Will to Power

I start by asking the group what they think of the story of the young Nietzsche lying in bed at night haunted by the dark power of sin. Do they think that is a good thing or a bad thing?

Nobody is quite sure how they are expected to reply to this. Rowan, a 12-year-old who hasn't joined the conversation so far, ventures that he sometimes thinks about what it must be like in hell at night. Rosamond cuts him off. 'I think it's child abuse,' she says. 'His church must have been a really scary place.'

Can they imagine what the pastor at his church must have been like?

'I imagine him doing two-hour sermons about hell-fire and then going home with saliva all over his beard to beat his wife, his children, his dog. He must have been very scary,' Rosamond continues.

I say that seems to go a bit far. Perhaps I should put the question another way. Did they think that Nietzsche's pastor enjoyed the power he had over his congregation?

They are still not sure of what I am trying to get at. I explain that I don't think that the Church is exempt from Nietzsche's idea of the will to power. I dig up a quote I had written down in my crib notes from Nietzsche's later book, *Beyond Good and Evil* about how every organisation which is not moribund has 'a will to grow, to gain ground, to ascendancy, not owing to any morality or immorality, but because it lives and because life is precisely the will to power.[46]

George gets my drift. 'So what you are trying to say is that the Church and the people in it also have the will to power. They want to make people agree with them and oppress those who don't. I think you are trying to say that Nietzsche's pastor, or whatever they call them in the Lutheran Church, probably loved the idea that everyone was afraid of him and his God. It made him feel powerful. I get that, but I don't get what that means for Christianity. Are you saying it is all a power trip?'

I say I think that what Nietzsche says about the will to power being in every living thing and in every organisation of living things is probably true. Everyone wants to grow in themselves and to make the world more to their liking. The Church wants this as much as anyone else. That is why it does all the bad things that Harry was concerned about.

'I don't like it,' says Freya, frowning heavily. 'Why are we here then if it is all badness?'

Because that wasn't really what Jesus was about. Nietzsche understood that. In one of the last books that he wrote before he went mad, he wrote: 'there was only one true Christian, and he died on the cross'.[47] What he meant was that we, as a Church, have never been true to Jesus' message which was to resist the will to power. I dig into to my crib notes to find another quote from *The Antichrist* to explain Nietzsche's position and read it out: 'What the Gospels make instinctive is precisely the reverse of all heroic struggle, of all taste for conflict. The very incapacity for resistance is here converted into something moral: ("resist not evil!" — the most profound sentence in the Gospels, perhaps the true key to them), to wit, the blessedness of peace, of gentleness, the inability to be an enemy'.[48]

There is a short silence. At last I think they can see where I am coming from. 'So you are trying to say that Jesus was good but the Church is bad?' asks Rosamond.

I say that I think that will to power is a problem for everyone. If everyone is wanting more power for themselves and their group, then the world will be a horrible place. Jesus's message is absolutely against that. He says things like 'the first shall be last' and 'who ever seeks to save his life will lose it', which I take to mean we should not allow ourselves to be driven by the will to power.

'That doesn't really explain why we should come to church though,' Rosamond continues, but before I can put together an answer Freya comes in with a left field question.

'Do you think God has the will to power?'

I guess so, I say, but then ask what she was thinking.

'If everything has the will to power, does God also? And is that bad or good?'

I am not sure whether this is a red herring or a genuinely interesting line of thought. Before I can continue, George comes to the rescue.

'I am not sure whether this is what she was thinking, but you said earlier that we got this sense of God from the idea that we are interconnected. Nietzsche seems to be saying that interconnected things have the will to power, so maybe what we are trying to do in church is be part of God's will to power.'

You mean that we are here to help the whole of life on earth flourish. It is a nice idea. Perhaps that is why we say in the

Lord's prayer 'Thine be the kingdom, the power and the glory forever and ever.'

'But it doesn't make things better,' Harry reminds us.

OK, I say, how about this. We come to church because we think Jesus' teachings are a good way of understanding the will of God and because this feeling of being interconnected is part of what we are trying to express through religion. That said Church isn't perfect because its will to power sometimes diverges from God's. This is particularly the case when it comes up against other religions or when its leaders feel the need for power over their flocks. Nevertheless, the Church has had some great leaders who have surely taken us closer to God. I mention two who have particular connections with St Mary's: Dietrich Bonhoeffer, the German Lutheran priest who was killed by the Nazis and Desmond Tutu, the Anglican archbishop of Cape Town who stood up against apartheid.

'That sounds reasonable,' says Rosamond, 'But it doesn't really say what the Church should do when it comes up against another religion. Can you tell us what your answer to his question about whether he might equally well have grown up a Muslim if he had been born into a different family?'

I say I think that Nietzsche got two things wrong. First, I think it is probably best to turn the question around. Surely it is more extraordinary that so many people have a sense of God all over the world than it is that there are different Gods. He shouldn't be unnerved by the possibility of believing in a different God. Second, I think that he didn't read the small print on the box named God. It says: 'Warning: may not be fully known'. I think he was so certain that he understood God in every detail that when he came across a question he didn't have an answer for, he began to doubt everything.

'So do you mean that all the religions are the same really?'

Sort of. I think it is in the nature of revelation that God is never fully apparent. It is a feature, not a bug in the system.

It expresses something important our relationship with God. It seems to imply that the religious life should be more about the pursuit rather than the capture.

'Like Nietzsche's parable of the tune?' puts in Rosamond.

How do you mean?

'I liked the bit you said about the end of a melody not being its goal.'

I agree that Nietzsche seemed to understand this. Zarathustra talks about a continuous process of self-overcoming, a going across, a bridge not a goal. He sees redemption not in the realisation of the God-like Superman, but in the dance that leads him towards it.

'But you haven't answered the question,' Harry points out. 'Do you think all religions are really worshipping the same God? In which case shouldn't we be going to the mosque instead?'

I say I don't know. I think many people in our part of the Church of England accept universal salvation: the idea that everyone will eventually be reconciled with God. The Church is always so mealy-mouthed about other religions. It thinks it is right but it doesn't want to offend other religions.

'What do you think?' asks Harry.

I think that everyone, even in the University Church, is worshipping a different God.

'Why is that?'

Before I can answer my wife comes into the room to say it is time to return to the service. The question of whether we are all worshipping one God or lots of Gods will be addressed in the next chapter.

Conclusion

There has been a long debate in physics about the basic nature of matter. When you break it down to its smallest components, do you find everything is made of particles or do you find it is made of waves? The question grows out of the fact that we are running out of readily understandable metaphors that we can use to visualise what the maths is telling us. It is also a question that goes to the heart of Nietzsche's understanding of the world.

We think of a particle as a little ball; something quite self-contained. Waves, on the other hand, don't really exist on their own. They are disturbances in something else, like water or an electromagnetic field.

Nietzsche's whole philosophy was based on the idea that we, as humans, are ultimately particles.[49] We are self-contained and we should live our lives in realisation of that fact. The religious condition, meanwhile, is a profound sense that we are waves. We are part of something much larger than ourselves and we should endeavour to live in harmony with that thing.

Nietzsche's case for being a particle is that that is how we experience life. We live as a distinct entity whose world begins and ends with us. We should make the most of this condition by removing the obstacles to our will.

Religion's case for the wave is that we don't really have any existence on our own. Who we are and what we want is shaped by our relationships and interactions with those around us. When we realise this, we see the need to live in a way which embraces our interconnectedness in the broadest possible way. For Christians this way is love; for Muslims it is peace; for Hindus and Buddhists it is the concept of Dharma.

Nietzsche was a sceptic. His experience of religion was that it is full of 'thou shalt not' commandments. It looks like the pursuit of power by other means. He may be right. Religion can provide the satisfactions of power. But does that make religion intrinsically wrong?

It seems that Nietzsche himself was not entirely convinced.

Unwittingly, Nietzsche also manages to convey the idea that we are waves. His writing subverts itself. For example, when Zarathustra laughs, it is never out of the joy of connecting with someone else's sense of humour. It is always because he sees a new way in which he has separated himself from the rest of humanity. It is difficult for readers to relate to this. It seems more like a howl of despair than an outburst of joy. Similarly, the songs Zarathustra sings about his love of eternity read like they were written by someone desperate to express an emotion he clearly didn't feel. Instead of affirming Zarathustra's philosophy, they seem to undermine it. Furthermore, it is difficult to ignore the fact that much of the book reads like a toxic male influencer Instagram feed. 'Man shall be trained for war, and woman for the recreation of the warrior: all else is folly,'[50] Zarathustra declares. But the picture accompanying the text of the feed is not of Zarathustra in his man cave surrounded by guns, fawning home boys, and half-naked women. It is of a lonely hermit trying to make small talk with his pets. It is as if Nietzsche is afraid of his own ideas.

And so he should be. A world in which people feel that they can detach themselves from any form of shared morality is scary. Jesus offered the antidote to the nihilistic struggle that grows out of it. Nietzsche seems to accept that but finds God unbelievable. In some ways he is right. We live the particle, but only imagine the wave. We should not believe in the wave simply because we are afraid of being a particle.

The next chapters of this book look at how God can become believable once again. For the moment, what I hope I have shown is that despite its flaws, religion can still be good.

Chapter 3

Jacques Derrida: *Writing and Difference*

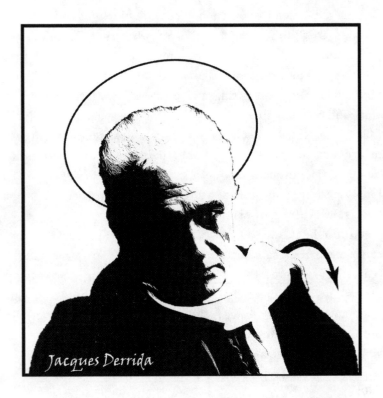

Jacques Derrida

How Do We Know God?

Introduction

Why is Jacques Derrida in this book? Hardly anyone outside academia has heard of him, and in academia people complain how difficult his books are to understand. The saying goes: 'If you think you have made sense of Derrida, then you probably haven't understood him'. He fancied himself as a philosopher, but he was never really taken seriously by the philosophical establishment. Literary theorists loved him, but since he died in

2004 he has fallen from fashion even in the literature departments of universities. He was not much of an atheist either. The best he could say of himself when pressed on the matter was: 'I rightly pass for an atheist'. Yet his work devastates religion.

That's because the focus of his writings was the way that we understand truth from texts. If you are looking for the weak link in the chain between man and God, it is in the texts we rely on to explain how religion works. I don't want to pick holes in other people's religions so I will focus on the Christian scripture here. Quite frankly it is a baffling mess. The Bible may be beautiful in parts, and inspiring too, but don't expect clarity. The twelfth century Jewish theologian, Maimonides, had the right word for it: perplexing. These are the most obvious difficulties with it:

1. **No one is agreed what is in it.** Different branches of Christianity have different views of which books are in the canon and which are not. Furthermore, the texts are untidy. Mark's Gospel has two possible endings. In one Jesus appears to the disciples after his body is found missing from the tomb; in the other his body is missing from the tomb, but there are no resurrection appearances.[51] It forces you as a reader to confront the frailty of the text at the very moment you most want certainty.

2. **It is translated.** We can never know how much is added or subtracted as the word of God moves from Hebrew and Greek to English. For example, in my New Revised Standard Edition, the sixth commandment is 'you shall not commit murder' with a little footnote adding: 'Or kill'. A lot of people have died in war because of that little bit of uncertainty.

3. **It is full of contradictions.** You can usually find a biblical authority for either side in any argument. Proverbs 26, verses 4 and 5 takes this to extremes. Verse 4 reads: 'Do not answer fools according to their folly, or you will be

a fool yourself'. Verse 5 reads: 'Answer fools according to their folly or they will be wise in their own eyes'. The Bible is simply not written in a way which gives rise to a single truth.

4. **It is inconsistent.** Both the Old and the New Testament contain multiple accounts of the same events and they don't add up. For example, Matthew relates Jesus to King David in 28 generations through Joseph, while Luke relates him to David through 42 generations to Mary. It is sort of possible, but why is Joseph involved if it was a Virgin birth?

5. **It is not clear what it is.** It is an odd mix of genres. The different books of the Bible encompass history, prophecy, devotional songs, poetry, law, and narrative storytelling. Some of the books of the Bible seem to give clear instructions about man's relationship with God, but not all of them. For example, the story of the destruction of Sodom and Gomorrah in the book of Genesis is often cited as evidence of God's dislike of homosexuality, but as guidance on sexual morality it is somewhat undermined by what happens next. Lot and his daughters escape the brimstone, but the latter then become afraid that there might be no other men in the world so get their father drunk and have sex with him. It is not clear when there is supposed to be a moral message in the narrative and when there is not.

6. **Its meaning is often deliberately unclear.** Jesus talks in puzzles and paradoxes, leaving his audience to decipher what he means. When asked why he speaks like this, his explanation doesn't make any more sense. 'To you it has been given to know the secrets of the kingdom of heaven, but to them it has not been given. For those you have, more will be given and they will have in abundance;

but from those who have nothing, even what they have will be taken away', Jesus says, before adding that this lack of clarity fulfils a prophecy of Isaiah.[52] It leaves the impression that we can never really be sure of anything we read in the Bible because it is pre-ordained that some of us will never get it.

All this adds up to the fact that the Bible is not like a set of flat-pack instructions from Ikea. It doesn't give clear directions in a universal language which will enable you to assemble your own personal stairway to heaven. What it gives you is a challenge of interpretation. The question 'how should we read the Bible?' ends up being more important in shaping the way we understand God than the question 'what does the Bible say?'

Take for example St Paul's letter to the Ephesians, chapter 6 verse 5:

'Slaves, obey your earthly master with fear and trembling, in singleness of heart, as you obey Christ; not only while being watched, In order to please them, but as slaves of Christ, doing the will of God from the heart.'

We can choose to read this literally. It would give the impression that God thinks that we should accept the injustices of this world, including slavery. Those who bear suffering with fortitude will be rewarded in the next world. But we can also choose to read the passage metaphorically. In that case Paul is suggesting that we should live as if we are slaves of Christ. Given that elsewhere in his letters[53] Paul says that in Christ there 'is no longer slave or free' and that we should 'not submit again to the yoke of slavery' it seems an equally valid interpretation. But who knows? America had a civil war to settle these theological niceties.

What this means is that before we can get to God in the Bible, we have to agree on an approach to reading it.[54] Or to put it another way: literary theory comes before God.

That is where Derrida comes in. He was probably the leading critical theorist of the twentieth century. By that, I mean that by the end of the century he had had more impact on the way academics think how reading works than anyone else. He was seen as a radical in the 1960s and 1970s, but by the 1980s his thinking permeated — and divided — humanities departments around the world.

The best way of understanding him is probably not as a radical, however. That gives people an excuse to dismiss him. Rather he should be seen as part of a long evolution in our understanding of the relationship between writer and reader, which has happened over the past couple of centuries. Historically the assumption was that the writer was the one in charge of meaning. The reader's job was trying to understand the author's intention. Over time, however, it has become increasingly obvious that readers bring a lot of baggage with them to each appointment with a book. This baggage informs how they understand it. This is as true of Jane Austen as it is of the Bible. Once a sensibility has been awakened, it can't be put back to sleep.

For example, a twenty-first-century reader cannot pretend that the Holocaust never happened when they read of Pilate washing his hands of responsibility for Jesus' death in Matthew's Gospel. Having been asked to free Barabbas rather than Jesus, the Jews cry: 'May his blood be on our hands and on our children'.[55] Today we can't read this verse without knowing the way in which it has been used to justify the crimes of antisemitism. It makes today's reader feel uncomfortable in a way that Matthew's original first-century audience would be puzzled to comprehend.

In that sense, it is not at all radical to say that the reader brings at least as much to a book as a writer. We bring all of the history and experience that lies between us and the author whenever we open a book. This isn't contentious when we are reading Jane Austen; it enriches the experience to imagine meanings in it that she could never have considered. Exploring the Bible in this way is much more controversial. The scripture is supposed to hold the key to understanding the one eternal God. Its message should not vary from age to age. Yet it does, and by extension it also differs from person to person. We all bring to it different personal histories and associations.

The Church has always been nervous of this. It has always wanted to say: 'this is how the Bible should be understood'. That is where its weakness lies. Christianity, like most religions, is built on a self-sealing argument. That is to say, if you accept its premises, then it is logically impervious to contradiction. It is one of the things that most infuriates atheists when arguing against believers.

Believer: 'There is life after death.'
Atheist: 'That is not possible.'
Believer: 'Yes it is. God can do impossible things.'
Atheist: ..,

Derrida said: 'il n'y a pas de hors-texte.' This is interpreted to mean that there is nothing outside of or in front of the text to tell you how it is supposed to be read or understood.[56] All possible readings are equally valid. He might have continued the discussion as follows:

Derrida: 'So how do you know that God can do impossible things?'
Believer: 'Because the Bible says so?'

Derrida: 'How do you know that is what the Bible means?'
Believer: ...

The reason I have chosen to include Derrida in this book is because his thinking is a challenge to the possibility of divine revelation through scripture. However, the paradox is that if we can accept that he may be right about the way reading works, we may in fact get a better understanding of God in the world.

Where Was He Coming From?

Derrida would hate this section. He felt we should focus on writers' ideas rather than their lives. This wasn't just a preference. It was also a central part of his philosophy. When you start trying to understand an author's work through their life, you erase most of the possible meanings of that work. There are so many other ways that a text can and should be understood. Furthermore, you are also bound to fail. You cannot know someone else's life as it is lived in flesh and blood. You can only know it through the writings and other traces it left. Finding the meaning of a book through the author's life, therefore, becomes a circular quest.

At the heart of Derrida's philosophy was the idea that we should not read a text in just one way. We should try to read it in every possible way. He called the process 'deconstruction'. The word is a kind of pun, bringing to mind both the idea of taking things apart, but also reversing the way we normally understand or 'construe' a text. It involves looking as much at what was left unsaid, as what was said: playing on the punning sounds of words and their associations; seizing on any ambiguities and double meanings; finding the traces of meaning left in words by the system of differences that define them. It doesn't end up with an understanding of the true meaning of a text. It ends up with a mess of multiple and often contradictory meanings. The whole process might sound like a waste of time; why read something if not to make sense of it? There is a logic to it, but it makes most sense in a historical context. Hence the need for a section in this chapter on where Derrida was coming from, whether he likes it or not.

The historical context of his life is that he was born in Algeria in July 1930. It was a world where the majority of people were ruled by White European males. He died in Paris in October 2004, in a world of diversity and self-determination. Between those two dates, the way we understood the world changed. It fragmented. Derrida provided a philosophy of this fragmentation. It could be used to pull apart the consensus, but it could also be used to explain a world without consensus.

This concept of fragmentation is important to understand, but it is also difficult to explain. It is important to this book too, because it wasn't just the White European males who lost out. The Church did as well. We will get on to that. The fragmentation is difficult to explain because it is self-referential. It applies to the process by which you understand what I am writing here. If everyone reading this could immediately understand it, then there wouldn't be fragmentation. There would be consensus. The fact is that some readers will immediately recognise what I am talking about. Others will be puzzled or insist I am wrong. There is no easy way of bridging the gap between these different perceptions.

Let's start then with this statement: 'the majority of people were ruled by White European males in 1930'. Is it a fact, or is it loaded with judgement? In 1930 you could just about have read it as a fact. Most books were written by and for White European males. The moral associations we now make with being a 'White European male' either did not exist or were suppressed. Since 1930, the meaning of the phrase has evolved in two different directions. Some people will read it as the starting point for a story on how the privilege and prejudice of the ruling elite was exposed and then vanquished in the post war years. Other people read it completely differently. For them 'White European male' are trigger words; a warning that they are likely to be coming across something that they disagree with. Both groups think that they have reason on their side. The former because it seems self-evident that the world should not be built around the comfort of a small, racial elite. It should be plural and diverse with everyone enjoying equality. The latter group — those who bridle at the phrase 'White European male' — don't feel that they are denying anyone equality. They don't think their values have grown out of their White male identity. They think that their values are universal and based on respect for blind justice and reason. They think the world has gone mad; it no longer accepts the basic truths that they grew up with. They see a stupid irony in being called racist simply because of the colour of their White skin.

This is the fragmentation in our understanding of the world since 1930. We have moved from a time when one big truth seemed possible, to one in which reasonable people can disagree fundamentally about the basic facts of the world and have no means of resolving their arguments. For example: who won the 2020 US election? What is a woman? When does life start?

What we think is true appears to be a function of our values and our perspective. This is a difficult idea to accept. If we step back from the world, we know this to be the case; it is the only explanation of these unresolvable questions. When we are in the thick of it, however, we fight for what we think is true. That is the nature of truth. We will defend it against those who say it is a lie.

It didn't work like that when Derrida was born in 1930. The values and perspectives of White European males were considered more valid than everyone else's. And these values and perspectives were self-affirming. Europeans were civilised. Others were savage. Europeans based their judgement on objective reason, while others relied on subjective emotion. They were cultured. Others were closer to nature. Europeans created wealth. Others perpetuated poverty. They believed in a universal religion, others had local pagan gods. This hierarchy seemed to be true because it was so successful. It had enabled White European males to colonise and control 70 per cent of the world. It is difficult to argue with the righteousness of a machine gun or the wretchedness of an empty stomach.

Derrida made his career picking apart this consensus of values and perspectives. He did it through textual criticism, because the way we understand words holds the key to the way we understand the world. When he deconstructed a text, he looked out for its implicit value judgements. He called these 'binary oppositions' and they included some of the pairs mentioned above: civilisation/savage; culture/nature; White/ Black; reason/emotion. Derrida also looked at the perspectives. What was centred? What was marginal? That was why he wasn't bothered that he didn't end up with the true meaning of the text. For him the true meaning of a text was in the pile of shredded and senseless ideas left behind when you really started questioning the assumptions of western thought. It meant that what we understand as truth, is in fact an unstable and partial view.

Derrida was successful because history was on his side. It pulled apart the prejudices of the White European male consensus more effectively than any literary theorist. After the Holocaust, who can claim to be civilised and who can claim to be savage? The civil rights movement, bloody wars of decolonisation, women's liberation — all challenged the White European male perspective that had ruled for the previous 400 years.

Derrida's own perspective gave his arguments an authenticity which was difficult to deny.

In 1930, Algeria was not a French colony but a department of France. Derrida's parents were assimilated Sephardic Jews. They had French citizenship (unlike the majority Muslim population, who did not). In 1940, however, when France fell to the Nazis and the Vichy regime took charge of Algeria, Algeria's Jews lost their citizenship. The 14-year-old Jacques Derrida was excluded from school as a result of his ethnicity in 1942.

It was a radio broadcast in 1948 with Albert Camus that inspired the young Derrida to become a philosopher. He left Algeria in 1949 to prepare for the entrance exams for the oldest of France's elite Grandes Ecoles: the Ecole Normale Supérieure. He was eventually successful and so began his career in academia. This journey from exclusion at the troubled margins of French society to its intellectual heart is a good simile for the 'recentring' that Derrida liked to achieve through the practice of deconstruction.

Although successful enough as a philosophy teacher, first at the Sorbonne then, in 1964, back at the Ecole Normale Supérieure, his big break came in October 1967 when he was invited to give a paper at Johns Hopkins University in Baltimore. There will be more about his paper in the next section. The important point here is to say that it turned him into an academic superstar who was lauded with honours until the end of his life in 2003.

In contrast to Derrida, the Church fared less well as the world became more questioning of established hierarchies. It was so tightly knotted up in the White European male perspective that its values seemed indistinguishable.

Where, for example, did we get the idea that men should have a superior public role than women? Did it come from an old cultural assumption that women should look after the family or did it come from 1 Corinthians 11, verse 3: 'I want you to understand that Christ is the head of every man, and the husband is the head of his wife?' Similarly, was the acceptance of slavery and the condemnation of homosexuality something that came from culture or religion?

It matters because Christianity set itself up above other religions on the basis of its universality. While other religions are content to minister to their own people, Christianity burns with an evangelical zeal. It is the Good News. It is the Way. The spread of the Word from first-century Judaea to the four corners of the world is as much a part of the Christian story as a baby in a manger.

It means that Christianity has been so tied up with colonialism as to be indistinguishable. Who can say who was the greatest Christian missionary? Was it David Livingstone who brought the Gospel to the heart of Africa? Or was it Benjamin Robins, the author of the *New Principles of Gunnery* (1742), whose understanding of ballistics gave Europeans a long-standing military advantage over indigenous armies in the Americas, Asia and Africa?

While Christianity was the largest and fastest growing religion in the world, there was little urgency to questions about its inclusivity, its arrogance towards other religions, and its relationship with the uglier side of nineteenth- and twentieth-century politics. The numbers spoke for themselves. Then the music stopped.

Values changed. For a younger generation of liberals, 'universal' values such as inclusivity and freedom of conscience looked like a better moral choice than the values that their parents may have got from the Church. Conservatives, on the other hand, became more wedded to the cultural aspects of Christianity, such as the inferior role of women and the suppression of homosexuality. People stopped going to Church in Europe, and Christianity lost its overall narrative of inevitability. To more and more people, Christianity has begun to look like a pile of shredded and senseless ideas rather than a universal and absolute truth.

This is where I think Derrida can help.

He may have thought that absolute and universal truth existed. He just didn't think we could reach it. All we experience is text — a wall of words. These words shape our thoughts, but they are fickle. They are playful and ambiguous; they have tangled and often contradictory layers of meaning which seem to be constantly shifting. It seems to me that anyone who has read the Bible will recognise this and agree. That is why I have included Derrida in this book. Although he was what passed for an atheist, and some of what he said is very challenging for Christians, he can help us understand how and why we do and don't understand the Bible. In this post-colonial, post-truth world this can give us a sharper view of God.

Sidebar: Out of the Margins: Where's the Diversity in This Book?

How should you understand this book as you read it now? Derrida would ask you first to question what is centred in it? What has been pushed to the margins? Even the determinedly unobservant will notice that it is written by a man about the anti-religious thoughts of four men. All of them are White as well. If I were Jacques Derrida, I might say that by centring the White and the male in this way, I am inviting the reader to recover a parallel Black and female narrative from the margins. That unwritten narrative might be more compelling than the one I have, in fact, written.

More practically I could bring some other voices into this chapter: Hélène Cixous and Julia Kristeva immediately come to mind. Both made important contributions to the post-structuralist movement with which Derrida was associated in the 1960s and 1970s. Like Derrida, they challenged the academic consensus that language and culture had a universal structure underlying it. They believed that the structures that underpinned society were much more fluid and political than the ones structuralists would accept. Cixous challenged what she saw as the patriarchal structures of society from a feminist angle. She argued that women's writing, like their bodies, had been objectified and controlled by men. Like Derrida, she was an Algerian-born Jew. She didn't write much about God, but nevertheless her line of thinking is also a big challenge for religion. If scripture is largely written by men, and it has largely given rise to religious institutions that empower men, what is the basis for believing in an inclusive God?

Julia Kristeva also wrote from a feminist standpoint, but she also had a broader contribution to make to the post-structuralist movement. While others focused on challenging or tearing down what they saw as subconscious or embedded power structures of society, she was interested in exploring the world beyond structure. She trained as a psychoanalyst and wrote about the developing sense of self in young children and the importance of the rhythmic, affective and bodily aspects of language that they discover before they understand its meaning. More relevant to this book is her work on intertextuality. She made the point that all texts refer to other texts. In a large way that is how they get their meaning. When any writer uses the words 'good' or 'evil' they are inevitably referring, in part, to the meaning of those words established in the Bible. In that sense you could say that the Bible permeates the whole of western literature. The problem comes when you realise that the relationship works both ways. When we go back to reading the Bible, after reading a novel which talks about good and evil, we inevitably bring those references back to the Bible. It means that, over time, the secular world has completely permeated our understanding of the Bible. It means that the Bible doesn't tell us of the God of Abraham and the Apostles anymore. It tells us of a God that is defined by the sum of everything we have read in contemporary media. That God is marginal, impotent, and perhaps non-existent.

I could write chapters of this book on both Cixous and Kristeva, but I have chosen Derrida. He is better known and I can use his name as a signifier of all the ideas that came out of the post-structuralist movement in a way that I couldn't so easily with Cixous or Kristeva. He was also more directly interested in religion. I think he would feel ambivalent about this honour. On the one hand he was very much the alpha male. He dominated university seminar rooms for three decades, mixing charm with a quick wit, provocative repartee and plenty of sexual puns. He delighted in words like 'dissemination' which could mean both the process of spreading ideas, and the expulsion of semen. On the other hand, Derrida would also realise that by centring him in this way, I am inviting the reader to depose him and replace him with thinkers on the margins.

What Was His Big Idea?

Derrida was bubbling with them, but most of them don't have much relevance for this book. We will look at two which are most directly a challenge to religions which look to scripture as their inspiration.

Turtles All the Way Down

Stephen Hawking opens *A Brief History of Time* with the following anecdote:

'A well-known scientist (some say it was Bertrand Russell) once gave a public lecture on astronomy. He described how the earth orbits around the sun and how the sun, in turn, orbits around the centre of a vast collection of stars called our galaxy. At the end of the lecture, a little old lady at the back of the room got up and said: "What you have told us is rubbish. The world is really a flat plate supported on the back of a giant tortoise". The scientist gave a superior smile before replying, "What is the tortoise standing on?" "You're very clever, young man, very clever," said the old lady. "But it's turtles all the way down!"

Most people nowadays would find the picture of our universe as an infinite tower or turtles rather ridiculous. But why should we think we know better?'[57]

Derrida would be quite content with an infinite tower of turtles. His big insight into the way that language works is that truth is infinitely deferred. To understand the how and why of that we need go back into history a bit.

Until the twentieth century, most people thought that words got their meaning from the things they represent. This idea is often ascribed to Plato, but in fact it comes from generations of parents frantically mouthing the words 'mama' or 'dada' while pointing at themselves in the hopes that they will be the first to be recognised by their confused offspring. This might be the way that very young children get to understand that words refer to things, but it has an obvious flaw. Most words are quite abstract, and even those words which are concrete need a bit of thinking about before they can be applied correctly. For example, how do you go from understanding who your mama and dada are to understanding who their mamas and dadas might be?

The Swiss linguist, Ferdinand de Saussure (1857–1913), came up with an alternative explanation of how words give meaning. He proposed that we understand their meaning from the way they are used in relation to each other. For example, if someone uses the word 'mother' I don't understand what is meant by connecting it in my mind to the various actual mothers I have come across. I understand it by knowing that a mother is in the category of family relations and it is not the same as father or daughter.

Another way of understanding what Saussure was trying to say is to think of language as being a bit like maths. When we do sums like six times seven, we don't work it out by thinking of six things (like cats) which might have seven other things (like kittens), then try to count the number of kittens. We work it out by knowing the relationship between six and seven, and never really leaving the realm of numbers in order to work out the answer.

The fact that words do not get their meaning directly from things but from their relation to each other seems obvious when you think about it. If words did refer directly to things, then there should be a direct one-to-one relationship between words and the things they represent in every language. Anyone who has studied foreign languages will know that very few words have exact translations. Mostly there is a mismatch. For example, the word for both 'bored' and 'annoyed' is *ennuyé* in French. If boredom is a real thing and annoyance is a real thing, then there should be separate words for them each of them in every language. That there isn't suggests that words don't map directly on to reality.

That is not the end of it. Once you realise that French people use the same word for being bored and being annoyed, you start to wander whether the French find boredom more annoying than the English speakers. From there you might start to worry how much your thoughts are altogether shaped by language.

Can we think without words? If we can, it is almost a moot point. We can only express our thoughts in words. Who is to say that the important bit of thinking is not done in language?

This idea that language shapes our thoughts and our thoughts shape our culture became one of the most important -isms of twentieth-century academia: structuralism. This suggested that the objective of the study of the humanities should be to uncover the hidden patterns in myths, rituals and other cultural expressions to understand the deep structure that might lie beneath.

Derrida was dubious.

He agreed that language shapes thought, but he didn't think that this created a firm structure into which you could read any great truths about society. That is because language doesn't have a definite structure. It has an indefinite one. This is where it becomes turtles all the way down.

A nice summary of Derrida's thinking is the phrase: 'Words mean through differing, but through differing they defer meaning'.

What is meant by this is that when we start thinking about the meaning of words, we don't have to stop when we think we have grasped the meaning. We can go on for ever. The example of this that is often given is the idea that you can look up a word in a dictionary and find that the definition is made up of other words, and when you look up the meaning of those words, they take you on to other words, and so on. You may eventually get back to the word you started with, but at no point do you ever get to a point of complete clarity.

However, that illustration doesn't quite capture the breadth of the point that Derrida is trying to make. Take the sentence 'I believe in God'. It might, on the surface, sound like a simple profession of faith, but at the same time it seems to contain an element of doubt. The fact that you are having to say it suggests that there is some uncertainty. This word 'believe' is defined as the opposite of 'doubt', so in a way whenever someone uses the word 'belief' the possibility of the opposite also goes through one's mind.

Obviously there needs to be a high degree of commonality in what we understand by words in order that language can function as a means of communication. At the same time, if we are not aware of all the possible ways in which a word or phrase might be understood, we would probably find ourselves unable to understand anything. We must parse the context of what is said in order to get an idea of its likely meaning. A word like 'believe' means almost nothing when it is on its own, but a million different things when it is used in a sentence.

There may be some people who feel that it is enough for people to 'get what I mean' when they use a word, and that any concerns that meaning is not definitive are just academic quibbles. It is not as simple as that. The meaning of words changes over time, whether or not the actual definition changes. Our references change. I once heard this summed up in the following quote: 'The writers of the New Testament had almost certainly read Shakespeare, Marx and Virginia Woolf'. It sounds topsy-turvy but it makes a good point. There is no real way of telling whether we are reading a meaning into a text because it was put there by the writer or because it was put there by the references that we might bring to reading it. Again, when you start contemplating these possibilities you don't get to a finite end point. You just get turtles all the way down.

This is great news if you are exploring the richness of literature, but it spells trouble if you are reading the Bible and expecting to find a revelation of God's ultimate truth.

The Transcendental Signified

This is a horrible phrase. It is a warning to any readers who might be inspired by this book to read Derrida in the original. Most of his writing uses jargon like this. He usually leavens this technical vocabulary with erudite puns so there is some reward for perseverance. There is no jokey payoff for understanding what the 'transcendental signified' is, but it is important to tackle it in this book because it is essentially another name for God.

Derrida himself defined the 'transcendental signified' as 'that which, being itself unrepresentable, governs the substitution of all other signs and signifiers in a signifying chain'.[58] You could think of it as the source code or operating system in a computer: the basic truth that defines all other truths. Alternatively, you could just read the beginning of St John's Gospel: 'In the beginning was the Word, and the Word was with God, and the Word was God'. Word is the English translation of the Greek *logos* which in the original Greek can mean 'reason' or 'law' as well as 'word'. It creates this idea that at the centre of things there ought to be a Horcrux or an Infinity Stone that underpins everything else.

Derrida's point is that we can never reach this transcendental signified because meaning is always deferred. It is turtles all the way down. Instead, what we get is a yearning for 'presence'.

This concept of presence goes back to Derrida's big beef with the structuralists. They felt that speech was a better source of truth than writing. Writing was invented later than speaking, they argued, and at best it was just a representation of speech. At worse it was a cause of confusion because without the speaker being there to ensure that writing was properly understood, it will always be misinterpreted.

Derrida profoundly disagreed with the idea that speech was any more authentic than writing. In fact, it was his attack on this structuralist idea in a paper he gave at Johns Hopkins University in Baltimore in October 1966 (and published in *Writing and Difference*) that propelled him to superstardom. He felt that words gave meaning in exactly the same way, whether they were spoken or written. Furthermore, this yearning for the presence of the author was in fact a yearning for a definitive truth that could never exist. The presence of God is necessarily an absent presence, Derrida concluded.

One can sort of see where he is coming from. Imagine being a Martian and being given a copy of the Bible to read: 'In the beginning God created the heavens and the earth'. Your first question is 'who is this God bloke?' You don't have anything else to go on (remember Derrida says 'il n'y a pas de hors-texte'), so you keep on reading. Initially God says and does a lot of things; later on in the Bible he becomes more distant and abstract. You can't come away feeling that you have actually touched God. What you have is an understanding of a character in a book, and a yearning for presence: for God to be actually there to make it all real.

Derrida was careful not to say categorically that God did not exist. In Derrida's roundabout logic, disproving the existence of God entails the possibility of proving the existence of God. He didn't want to concede as much as that. Anyway, he was not a big fan of religion. He thought it was the source of many of the binary oppositions he despised so much.

Sidebar: What Did Aslan Say?

Derrida was not the only philosopher to highlight the perfidy of language in the twentieth century. Bertrand Russell and Ludwig Wittgenstein were already on the case in Cambridge before World War I. 'Philosophical problems arise when language goes on holiday,' Wittgenstein remarked. The two of them believed that many philosophical problems were in fact tricks of language that could be solved by being a lot more careful how they used words. Russell even tried (and failed) to create his own entirely logical and unambiguous language. Wittgenstein meanwhile wrote his most famous work, the *Tractatus Logico-Philosophicus*, in the form of 525 sparely written, hierarchically numbered statements, lest he be tricked by the perfidy of language at any point.

For the analytical school of philosophy of which Russell and Wittgenstein were among the founders, Derrida was a complete anathema. When the University of Cambridge offered the French philosopher an honorary degree in 1992, a group of them signed a letter to *The Times* newspaper complaining that Derrida's work as a philosopher 'did not reach the required standards and vigour'. They went on to suggest that Derrida's works 'seemed to consist in no small part of elaborate jokes and puns ("logical phallusies" and the like) and M. Derrida seems to us to have come close to making a career out of what we regard as translating into the academic sphere tricks and gimmicks similar to those of the Dadaists or of the concrete poets'.

In some ways the analytical philosophers and Derrida were talking at cross purposes. The former wanted to strip language of its capacity for confusion whereas Derrida wanted to luxuriate in that confusion. Nevertheless, Wittgenstein did come up with some ideas which are relevant to this chapter's big question: how do we know God?

'If a lion could speak we would not understand him', he argued. The lion's view of the world — and its reference points — are so different from our own that we could not relate to anything it said, Wittgenstein thought. 'To imagine a language is to imagine a form of life,' he said.

It takes one back to Aslan, the lion in C. S. Lewis' Narnia. How come the children were able to understand him so well? If God could talk, would we be able to understand him?

Where Is God in Derrida's *Writing and Difference*?

In this book I have tried to focus the discussion on a single book written by each of my four authors. For Derrida, I have selected *Writing and Difference*, although I have barely mentioned it in the text so far. The book, a collection of essays published in 1967, includes the paper *Structure, Sign and Play in the Discourse of the Humanities*, in which he launched his attack on the structuralist orthodoxy and thus established his reputation. It doesn't talk as much about God as *On Grammatology* which he also published in 1967, but it does establish the basics of his thinking. I doubt anyone would read it for fun, least of all a group of teenagers. Nevertheless, our discussion group did find the ideas in it engaging when I explained the book to them one Sunday soon after Easter.

I began with the question that I think we need an answer to: how do we know God?

There is confusion. 'What do you mean? Through the Bible?' Rosamond eventually asks.

Ok, through the Bible, I say.

'Well you might mean not through the Bible, like a vision or something.'

They seem to be sensing a trap. I say through the Bible again.

It doesn't get us anywhere. So I try another approach. What do they think of the day's Gospel reading? It is the story of doubting Thomas.

'I think it is weird. Why don't any of the disciples just ask Jesus what happened when he shows up?' James, a 13-year-old with a good line in scepticism, asks.

'Maybe it is supposed to be kept a mystery. If Jesus explained it then perhaps it wouldn't seem so amazing,' suggests Rosamond.

'That still doesn't make sense. The Gospel writer seems pretty uninterested in what everyone else is going to have to build their faith on. I'm not surprised Thomas was doubtful,' James continues.

Harry joins in. 'What I don't get is why it says in the story that the doors are locked against the Jews and then Jesus appears all flesh and blood with his wounds gaping open. Are they trying to say that Jesus was like a spirit who could walk through doors or are they saying he was like some sort of zombie who still had a body that obeyed the laws of physics?'

'I know this one,' pipes up Rowan. 'The vicar from our old church explained it. He said Jesus when he was resurrected, was like, super-real. He could pass through doors like aeroplanes pass through clouds.' Nobody thinks this is a sensible explanation.

'That still doesn't explain whether the idea is that Jesus is a ghost, a zombie, Iron Man or what after the resurrection,' Harry reminds us.

Freya, the youngest member of the group, then cuts in with a left field question: 'Do you think Jesus smelled?'

How do you mean?

'Freya is obsessed with these things,' her sister Marion explains. 'Do you know what she asked the other day? She asked our mother: "Did Jesus poo?"'

Everyone looks at Freya.

'It is a good question,' she insists. 'I was wondering why people never do poos in stories or on television, even though we have to do them every day and it's boring. It made me think that stories, even true life stories, are not trying to tell you what actually happened. They are trying to tell you the story. That's why I wanted to know whether Jesus pooed.'

Did you get an answer?

'No, they were all laughing too much. I think he must have when he was alive because he was a real person, but I don't know what happened after the resurrection. Maybe he didn't need to, but then he did have fish for breakfast one day and he was around for forty days.'

The others are all laughing now, I am worried that we are getting a very long way from what we are supposed to be talking about. Harry's older brother, George, then joins the conversation. 'I think the point is that we can't know. As soon as we start trying to explain the resurrection, we have to imagine bits of the story that aren't there, and that's making it up.'

Do you mean we have to take Bible stories at face value, rather than trying to break through the surface of them to imagine what actually happened?

'I think that is probably what Derrida is trying to say. Even if we do try to imagine different ways in which the resurrection happened, we can never be sure of any of them. They just float around in our heads. We can never get to the actual Jesus behind them.'

'That sounds rather convenient to me,' Harry puts in. 'We can't doubt anything in the Bible because whenever something unlikely happens we just have to say: "That's the story and we can't go behind the text".'

'I think it cuts both ways,' explains George. 'We can't doubt it or be sure of it, that is what Derrida is trying to say.'

'Do you think it matters?' Rosamond is asking me.

I reply that my father once told me that complaining that the Bible isn't true is like complaining that the Mona Lisa isn't true. I say that I think he was trying to say that it is art. It is made of words like the Mona Lisa is made of paint.

Rowan then rejoins the discussion. 'I am thinking of Harry's idea of all the different ways that Jesus might be after the resurrection: ghost, zombie, Iron Man, even Freya's pooey Jesus. If everyone is imagining him in a different way, does that mean that everyone believes in Jesus in a different way?'

I say that this is the point I made at the end of the Nietzsche discussion. We all believe in different Gods.

'Doesn't that defeat the point of Christianity?' Rosamond asks. 'Isn't there supposed to be just one God?'

I think that there is just one God, but it is impossible for us to know Him or Her. There is just too much to understand. We can read the Bible, but every time we read it we come away with something different. It is not written to be clear. As I mentioned before. That is a feature not a bug. It is written to intrigue and to engross.

'So where does that leave doctrine?' asks Rosamond. 'People died for things like transubstantiation even in this very Church,[59] and now you are saying it's all just words?'

I don't say it, but I am not sure whether I should be setting fire to centuries of formulations of Christian belief this morning. Nevertheless, I push on with this line of thinking to see where it ends.

That is the point, I say. If everyone accepted that words meant different things at different times to different people, there would be a lot less killing in this world.

'But what would the religion be if there was no creed or anything to say what you are supposed to believe?' Rosamond continues.

I continue to ad lib. I didn't say that we shouldn't have doctrine. I think it is a good record of how people understood things at a particular time, and that is helpful, but the idea that you can police the way people understand words is crazy. Think about the Nicene Creed. What does it mean when you say Jesus is of 'one substance' with the father. What is this substance?

'I thought it was trying to say that part of the same entity,' Rosamond replies.

But what is the substance?

'I don't know. Some sort of God stuff.'

Is it a physical or chemical substance?

'I don't know.'

Does anyone else know what this substance is?

'Maybe an illegal substance,' jokes Harry.

'Well it has got to be something that is both there and not there,' suggests Freya.

'So little theologian, has this substance got poo in it?' Marion asks, to tease her sister. 'Is God made of fishy breakfast poo?'

'I don't think I will ever be able to get that image out of my mind when I say the creed now,' James remarks.

'What about in communion when they say it is Jesus' body and it is those wholemeal wafers?' Harry begins. I am wary of where this is going but George is my saviour. He never gets drawn into the silliness the others in the group enjoy so much. I ask him his opinion on deconstruction and doctrine.

'I think doctrine has two purposes. One is to explore the meaning of God. The other is as some sort of membership test. I think using Derrida's deconstruction could be a good way of exploring the Creed as it might unpack new ideas about God. It does make the membership test rather difficult. You can't actually open up people's brains to make sure that they understand each word in the way they are meant to.'

'God can,' says Freya.

'That's true, but we're not talking about God here. We're talking about how the Church agrees what it stands for.'

'Don't you think though, that when they worked out all of this stuff, they decided on the meaning of all of the words first?' Rosamond suggests.

'I think if you were to ask a proper theologian you would get a better answer,' George explains, casting aspersions on my amateur credentials. 'They would probably be able to quote some early Church father who defined what "substance" actually meant, but then you would probably need another guy to come in and explain what his definition meant and so on. That is where it becomes turtles all the way down. And probably none of it makes sense to us now because so much is lost in translation from the Greek, and the meaning of words drifts over time anyway.'

'So why go to church?' George's younger brother, Harry, asks. 'You've got this room full of people all believing different things and no one really knows what anyone else is talking about. Isn't it just a pantomime.'

George doesn't have a ready answer. I say that it isn't a pantomime because what matters is that we all believe we are worshipping the same God even though our understanding of him or her might be very different. We come together to explore the mystery of this distant and incomprehensible thing of which we have a mystical sense, but do not know in any tangible way.

If God was fully apparent like the Highway Code, we probably wouldn't need to go to church. We would learn the signs and the rules and go about our lives not really thinking about them once we had understood them.

'So why don't you go to the Cowley Road mosque instead?' continues George.

I think all religions are trying to provide an answer to this feeling that there is something elusive and bigger than ourselves which provides purpose and meaning — and with which we should aim to live in harmony. However, different ideas of this thing resonate with different people in different ways. Personally, what resonates with me about Christianity is the idea that God can be human and can empathise with our experience. I also like the fact that there are four Gospels: it allows space for discussion. What resonates with me about Islam is the feeling of the incomprehensible enormity of God. I also think that the common experience of the Ramadan and the Hajj expresses the need for God to intrude into everyday life in a way that we don't get in Christianity. What I find more difficult about Islam is the idea that the Koran is the voice of God in Arabic and the very dogmatic approach to interpretation that it has engendered.

You could see religion as being a compulsion to sail across an unknown ocean to discover an unknown land. Different people have built different ships to make the journey; you are going to get into the one that looks to you the most seaworthy and best equipped, but you also don't know what the journey will bring. That means you can't necessarily make judgements about the other ships, especially as the whole enterprise is so unscientific.

'OK, so how do you answer your first question: "how do we know God?"'

I think I would agree with the orthodox Anglican answer here: through scripture, tradition and reason. That is to say, by looking at what humanity has said about its relationship with God in the past, and then applying our own reason and experience to come up with something that we can believe in with sincerity.

I think Derrida helps in all of this. Although he says it is impossible to reach an absolute truth like God through such a nebulous thing as language, I think he does capture the fluidity of our relationship with God and the infinite distance between God and humanity. These things are important in a changing world. They are also important in a world in which too much certainty can become a killer.

Conclusion

I would like to summarise my thoughts on Derrida with three quotations.

The first is attributed to St Francis of Assisi: 'Preach the Gospel every day. Use words if necessary'. It is a reminder that the primary commandment to Christians is to love. It doesn't matter how correctly we understand the Bible or Christian doctrine, Christians should distinguish themselves first of all through their love of the world and the people in it.

The second quote comes from St Paul's first letter to the Corinthians. In the King James version, it reads: 'For now we see through a glass, darkly; but then face to face'.[60] It is as if St Paul understood the impossibility of touching the face of God through writing long before Derrida. It is also a reminder that the ways in which we can come to know God in this world are fleeting, evanescent, mostly inexpressible and deeply personal. Revelation is like a scent on the wind or a something glinting in the distance that compels us to follow. This lack of solidity in revelation expresses something important about God, that we should take time to understand. It seems to imply that the religious life should be more about the pursuit rather than the capture.

The third quote comes from former Archbishop of Canterbury, Rowan Williams, in discussion with *His Dark Materials* author Philip Pullman. When the two met in a public discussion, Williams remarked 'We are talking about a set of historical events which have, as I would say by God's guidance, become the centre of a vastly complex imaginative scheme in which the whole of human history and human life gets reoriented'.[61]

I like the way that Williams describes Christianity as 'an imaginative scheme'. It is a reminder that our religion is a product of the human mind. It evolves with our imaginings. If we can no longer believe in a God who condones slavery, thinks that women should be subservient and other religions are bunk, then we will find ways of reading this into the Bible. The meaning of the words change as our sensibilities change.

For example, when we read in the Tenth Commandment that we should not covet our neighbour's 'male slave or female slave' or indeed 'his ox or ass' we have to follow Derrida's lead and question the assumptions of the text. It is our moral duty to look for the eternal message in the cultural wrapping paper in which it is presented. Is it OK to own slaves? Are slaves to be counted as chattels alongside oxen and asses? Should we assume that our neighbour who owns all this is a man rather than a woman? We have to engage our imagination to find answers to these questions. If we choose not to, then we seem to be imprisoning God in the past.

It may sound as if we are just loading onto God whatever faddish ethics with which we want to associate ourselves. We may also be accused of using the sophistry of language to slip out of some of the more improbable claims of the Bible. But it seems to be the only way that it is possible to believe in a living God. It is only if we engage our imaginations in the Christian story that it has, as Williams says, the power to reorient the whole of human history.

This last phrase brings to my mind the parable of the Pearl of Great Price. This is told concisely in Matthew's Gospel as follows:

'The kingdom of heaven is like a merchant in search of fine pearls; on finding one pearl of great value, he went and sold all that he had and bought it.'[62]

I think of the way the merchant might treasure this pearl, turning it over in his hands every day, looking for new depths in its prismatic sheen, enjoying the way its appearance changes in different light conditions, finding an ongoing satisfaction in his prize that collectors of other pearls might struggle to understand. It seems to me that this is the way we should treat the language of the Bible, continuously examining it to find new truths rather than believing that it has only one.

My objective in this chapter was to answer the question: how can we know God? The answer I find in Derrida's work is 'infinitely through our imaginations'. By infinitely I mean that we can never reach a conclusion. When I say 'through our imaginations' I mean that we should continually look for new possibilities in scripture and the world. It does mean that there are probably 8 billion different Gods imagined in the world today, and another 8 billion might be imagined tomorrow, but this is not a reason to disband churches. Rather, it should be a sign of the richness that might arise from sharing these imaginings.

Chapter 4

Stephen Hawking: *A Brief History of Time*

Stephen Hawking

Where Is God?

Introduction

In this chapter I am going to try to answer the question: where is God? For the physicist, Stephen Hawking, the answer is nowhere. He was an atheist. His objective in *A Brief History of Time* is to explain the beginning of the universe without the need for God. However, he did sow some confusion in the final words of the book when he suggested that if we can find a unified theory of the physics of the largest structures of the universe and that of subatomic particles 'we would know the mind of God'. He did not mean this literally. He meant it figuratively. 'I use "God" in an impersonal sense, like Einstein did, for the laws of nature; so knowing the mind of God is knowing the laws of nature,'[63] he explained in his 2018 book *Brief Answers to the Big Questions*.

The 2014 film of Hawking's life, *The Theory of Everything*, suggests another reason he chose to bring God into *A Brief History of Time*. It was to placate his first wife, Jane. Her Christian faith helped her through the emotional strain of caring for her husband as his physical health deteriorated. In the film he becomes quite cruel and egotistical as disease takes control of his body. The reference to God is presented as a recognition of her values and an apology for his behaviour. It also highlights the double meaning of this question 'where is God?' in the context of this book.

For Hawking the physicist, the question of the location of God is a physical one. If there is no place for God outside of the universe, and no sign of Him or Her inside of the universe, then God does not exist. For his ex-wife the question is a much more immediate and emotional one. Where is God in a world where you have two young children who need care and attention as well as a husband who cannot feed, wash or dress himself, and who in future will only become more dependent?

For Hawking the scientist, a God with whom one might have a personal relationship is wishful thinking. For his wife, however, the sort of God that Hawking seems intent on banishing is equally unpalatable. What is the point of a God who creates the universe and underpins the laws of physics, but doesn't have any connection with humanity?

Somehow, I think we need both types of God: the vast impersonal one which answers all the big questions about our existence, and the comforting human one who knows us intimately as individuals. This chapter is about the search for that God.

Where Is He Coming From?

Hawking hated the way people who didn't know him tried to make connections between his work and his life. It is unpleasant to speculate about how a motor neurone disease like the one Hawking suffered from might shape one's world view when one has no experience of his disease.

That's why I will use this section to address a broader issue: where is science coming from as it tries to answer questions about God? It is an important one as we move into the second half of this book. The first two authors we've covered — Nietzsche and Derrida — wrote about the non-existence of God from the point of view of the humanities. Hawking was a scientist and so is the subject of the next chapter, Richard Dawkins. It is a big change in mindset. The humanities like to argue things. The sciences like to prove them. Religion seems best able to hold its ground in the endless debates of the humanities. It struggles against the finality of science. It means that religious people need a way to resolve the nature of God with science. There are three main approaches:

1. God is right, science is wrong. This is the position of creationist Christians.
2. God is not detectable to science, but He occasionally intervenes to overturn science with a miracle. This is the position of most conservative Christians.
3. God exists on a different plain to science; the two never overlap. This is the position of many liberal Christians.

There is a fourth possibility which is the spirit of this book. It is that God and science are both fully overlapping and mutually compatible. It grows out of the idea there is nothing that we can learn about the world which doesn't tell us more about God.

In order to discuss these different possibilities, the first thing we have to do is establish what science is. It is a foreign language to the vast majority of people. The incomprehension it inspires makes it easier to dismiss. This incomprehension also means that most people miss out on the astonishing insights into the nature of the world that science can offer.

The best definition of science is that it is the marriage of mathematics and measurement. Each of these things on their own are mild curiosities, but together they become the human superpower. Their combination took our species from hunting and gathering in draughty caves all the way to the moon. The real power of science is the ability to predict how things will behave. This predictability follows from the fact that both maths and measurement are reliably true. Let me explain.

Maths on its own is abstract but, by definition, it cannot be wrong if it is done right. It is a set of rules applying to operations (e.g. plus, minus, times etc.) and values (e.g. numbers) that establish relationships (e.g. is equal to or is greater than). The same combination of operations and units always delivers the same relationships because all three are defined in a completely consistent way. That is the point of maths. There is no ambiguity.[64] It is a bit like chess in that sense. The rules make the game. Anyone — even God — who arbitrarily breaks the rules, is no longer playing the game. The difference between chess and maths is that the former is a game for two players, whereas pure maths is a game for one player. Its objective is to uncover the elegant and often outlandish patterns that can be created by the application of its rules to different combinations of values, operations and relationships. That makes pure maths a bit like playing with a kaleidoscope. Its joy comes from unexpected symmetries and patterns it generates.

Maths stops being a toy and becomes a superpower when the values fed into its equations are drawn from the real world. The patterns it then generates become predictions about the behaviour of the universe.

Measurement is the process by which we abstract data from nature, which can then be used in mathematics. It is also designed to be objectively true. A metre was originally defined as one 10 millionth of the distance from the equator to the north pole. Today, in order to ensure that it does not vary with any possible change in the shape of the world, it is defined by the distance light travels in a vacuum in one 299,792,458th of a second. The speed of light is an invariable constant of the universe. A metre is one of seven units (known as SI units) derived from universal constants which form the basis of all scientific measurements. The others measure time, mass, temperature, amount of substance, electric current, and light intensity. Neither man nor God can change any of them without running the risk that the whole universe would implode.[65] That is because a slight difference in any of them would upset the fundamental relationships which underpin the stability of basic building blocks of life and the universe.

Some see this as a proof of God's existence in itself. It seems to imply that everything in the world is so finely tuned for our comfort that it must have been designed for us by God. As we will see later in this section, this is not a good argument.

Much of practical science is devoted to ensuring entirely consistent conditions for measurement. Even so there is often some margin for error. This is not a fatal flaw. A degree of error relating to the accuracy of instrumentation can always be built into calculations to indicate the certainty with which a conclusion can be drawn. If errors arise which are not related to instrumentation and the way that it is operated, these are usually the first sign that we are not measuring what we thought we were measuring. It usually means that there is something more complex at work that needs to be understood. This improves the science rather than detracts from it.

Altogether it means that if one accepts the objective truth of maths, and the objective truth of measurement, then one also has to accept the objective truth of science.[66] The logic is inexorable, whether there is a God or no God.

Where religious people can find a weakness in science is in the question of what can be measured. Many of the things that really matter in life can't. Things like love, happiness, beauty, meaning, purpose, goodness can't be expressed in SI units. Prosaic people can try to rate these things on a numerical scale, but it rarely works well. Our feelings about these unmeasurable things ebb and flow and they are never easy to compare.

It means that most of the intelligent debate around science and religion is not about whether science tells us the 'truth' or not. Of course it does, in as much as it can. The real question is how these two worlds — the measured one and the unmeasurable one — intersect. You can find a good illustration of this quandary on the slopes of Mount Everest.

Two Approaches to Everest

The process of establishing that Everest is the highest mountain in the world started in 1802 when a 100-foot-long chain was laid out under a shaded canopy on a beach in Madras (now Chennai) in South India. The canopy was there to ensure that the heat of the sun didn't expand the metal links of the chain and throw the accuracy of the calculations. The chain became the baseline for a series of thousands of triangles that enabled The Great Trigonometrical Survey of India to measure the whole continent of India. The officers of the survey calculated distances and heights above sea level from point to point across the landscape until it reached the foothills of the Himalayas. From there it measured from peak to peak until the mountains became too hard to climb. In 1852 the mathematician, Radhanath Sikdar, confirmed that a summit, hitherto known only as peak XV, was 29,000 feet (8839 metres) above sea-level and the highest in the world. It was named Mount Everest after the former Surveyor General of India. It was an extraordinary feat of maths and measurement; Sikdar's number is only 29 feet short of the current calculation of the mountain's height using more accurate satellite measurements.

Sikdar himself is said never to have seen the mountain. He carried out his calculations in his office in Dehradun in the foothills of the Himalayas. His work did, however, inspire others to get closer to peak XV. Climbing it has become the proverbial pinnacle of thousands of people's ambitions.

One such person was a British engineer named David Sharp. He died on Mount Everest on 15 May 2006. His story opens out questions about ambition and purpose in life to which there is no measured answer. Sharp froze to death in what is known as Green Boots Cave at an elevation of around 8500 metres. He was an experienced climber and a purist. He had set out to climb the mountain on his own and without oxygen. He found himself overwhelmed in the so-called 'death zone'. This is where the atmosphere is too thin to support human life for long. As he knelt dying in the cave, some 40 other climbers passed him by. Most ignored him; some made perfunctory attempts to talk to him and to assess his condition. His only company in the cave was the long-dead owner of the eponymous Green Boots: the Indian climber, Tsewang Paljor, whose corpse had been left outside the cave since an expedition in 1996. Both Sharp's and Paljor's corpses have subsequently been moved out of sight of the main route to the summit. The bodies of a further 200 climbers remain frozen to the mountain slopes in the death zone today. They are too difficult to move without the risk of further loss of life.

The story shows how difficult it is to disentangle the 'what' questions that science is supposed to be equipped to answer from the 'why' questions it is not. Sikdar's feat of trigonometry explains why Sharp was in Green Boots Cave. What it doesn't explain is whether Sharp's goal was worth his life, or indeed whether Sharp's life was worth the goals of those other climbers who passed him by on their journey to the summit.

These are the questions of goodness, meaning and purpose which might be said to involve God. They are also questions which arise from the dilemmas of a physical world. How many of them would be asked if the measurable and the unmeasurable were not so tightly entangled? It means that in practice it is impossible to carve out separate worlds for science and religion, unless you want a God who leaves you alone with your destructive ambitions at 27,890 feet.

Sidebar: Uniting the Brain

So what matters: the data or the noise? Is it quantifiable things like physics and economics? Or is it the stuff you have to strip away in order to quantify them, such as emotion and individuality? If you feel in two minds as to the correct answer, you may be right. Each hemisphere of the brain takes a different side in this debate according to the psychiatrist and philosopher, Iain McGilchrist.

His study of the brain enabled him to build up a detailed picture of how the two halves of the brain work together, which he detailed in his book *The Master and His Emissary*.[67] He concludes that the right hemisphere experiences life as it is, in all its bewildering variety and fluidity. Its job is to understand the world, be vigilant towards threats and to assess potential mates and allies. It is also responsible for comprehending our humanity and the values such as truth, beauty, and goodness that go with it. The left hemisphere's job is to manipulate the world. It does this by simplifying everything into a model that it can work to get the job done. It likes certainty, categories, quantities, fixed things rather than fluid things. It sees the separate parts rather than the whole. It is responsible for precise language, although it tends to understand words in a very literal sense, missing irony and multi-layered meanings.

McGilchrist's central hypothesis is that the right brain is the real master of our lives, but the left brain is a control freak and a liar, which keeps trying to usurp the right. It is controlling because that it is the way it must think in order to get the job done. It is a liar because it is articulate, but doesn't know the limitations of its own intelligence. McGilchrist's fear is that left hemisphere thinking is steadily taking over the world, and thereby crushing our humanity.

He is not against science. In fact, he thinks that the breakthroughs achieved by truly great scientists like Albert Einstein are based on right hemisphere intuitions rather than the hard slog of the left brain's calculation and quantification. His concern is that if, as a society, we listen too much to the left brain, we will find our lives becoming more mechanical and tied down by petty rules. We will lose our appreciation of imagination, spontaneity, and emotional connection.

In his most recent book, *The Matter With Things*,[68] he takes this argument further, concluding with a chapter on 'The Sense of the Sacred'. In it he makes the case for the right brain's feeling of wonder about the world. It plants the seed of belief in the transcendent in our minds. He doesn't go as far as to saying that we have an in-built notion of God, but he does feel that we should feed this sense of wonder by opening our minds to it. He quotes Lao Tzu: 'The un-wanting soul sees what is hidden, and the ever-wanting soul sees only what it wants'.[69]

This sense of the sacred, that there is something larger and more important than ourselves at stake in our lives, is an anathema to the left brain. In McGilchrist's telling, this also makes it almost impossible to articulate. That is why religion is often so inexplicit about what is supposed to be most sacred to it. Instead, it talks in parables, poetry, music, icons, architecture — appealing to the right brain's imagination and its sense of beauty and goodness.

What Is the Big Idea?

A Brief History of Time aimed to connect the general public with the cutting edge of cosmology so that people could understand the origin of the universe. Yet I doubt that it would have sold 25 million copies if it had been about that alone. What makes it a compelling read is that Hawking has an agenda in telling the story of how scientists have been working towards a 'theory of everything'. It is that this theory, if it is correct, should have 'no boundary' and thereby do away with the need for God.

In maths and physics it is common to talk about 'boundary conditions' for a theory or equation. These either define the circumstances in which the theory works, or they define the initial set up that needs to be fed into the equation to define the subsequent outcomes. For example, the boundary condition of a game of Eight Ball Pool is that it is played with 15 balls on a rectangular table with pockets at each corner and the middle of each of the long sides.. Once those things are defined, you can use the physics of angular momentum to predict how the balls will move when a player makes a break.

Hawking's big breakthrough in thinking about the origin of the universe was that the only boundary condition should be that there are no boundary conditions. That is to say, the universe should be able to explain itself without the need for God, or anyone else, to define the initial set up or put limits on the extent to which the theory should apply.

Hawking first presented this No Boundary Proposal at a conference in the Vatican, staged by the Pontifical Academy of Sciences in 1981. It was a provocative place to unveil it. Pope John Paul II had organised the conference to demonstrate that the Catholic Church was no longer afraid of science, but he still had strong feelings about the dividing line between religion and physics. Opening the conference, the Pope said:

'Every scientific hypothesis about the origin of the world, such as the one that says that there is a basic atom from which the whole of the physical universe is derived (i.e. the Big Bang theory), leaves unanswered the problem concerning the beginning of the universe. By itself, science cannot resolve such a question: it requires human knowledge which rises above the physical, the astrophysical, what we call the metaphysical; what is required above all is the knowledge which comes from the revelation of God.'

This view has much in keeping with the theology of Thomas Aquinas (1225–1274). His two proofs of the existence of God were the 'unmoved mover' and the 'argument from first cause'. These are essentially two different ways of making the same point: you need God to explain the beginning of things. Hawking's point is that there is no need to imagine God striding out at the beginning of time, cue in hand, and slamming the white ball into the coloured ones to initiate the universe in a big bang. It could all have happened of its own accord thanks to the curious nature of quantum mechanics and relativity — the two theories which aim to explain how the universe works.

In many ways the No Boundary Proposal is a bigger threat to Christianity than Darwin's theory of evolution. Many Christians accept that God didn't make the world in seven days. What we find difficult to accept is that God had no role in creation at all. I include myself in that. When I ran the Sunday School for the younger children at the University Church and the reading of the week was the Creation story, the craft activity I devised for them had nothing to do with Adam and Eve. We decorated cards concealing cracker snaps. On the outside the children wrote: 'God made the world...'. When the card was opened, the snap fired off to reveal the words: 'with a Big Bang'. Since getting to grips with Hawking's No Boundary Proposal, I have had to consider the possibility that God wasn't needed for the Big Bang.

At the moment the No Boundary Proposal is just that: a proposal. That is because it only becomes credible once physicists have found a way of resolving quantum mechanics and relativity into a single unified theory which is mutually compatible. *A Brief History of Time* tells the story of how physicists have pursued this unification over the past 150 years.

As Christians we have to be prepared for the possibility that the No Boundary Proposal may be confirmed within our lifetime. It means that we have to make the effort to understand the physics of it. To the layperson, this physics seems wackier than the most outlandish religious cult beliefs. It is important to remember that all of it is built on the sober objectivity of mathematics and measurement.

Relativity: Two Bogglers and a Brain Blender

Relativity is the theory of how the big things in the universe work, developed by Albert Einstein in the first two decades of the last century. It has three main implications:

- **The faster you travel, the slower you get to the future**: This is because it turns out that the rate at which time passes is a function of how fast you are moving. For example, an astronaut on the International Space Station circling the earth at 17,135mph would find themselves to be 0.007 seconds younger than the people they left behind on earth after six months. At the speed of light (670,616,629mph) the passage of time grinds to a halt.[70] What this means is that it is better not to think of time as a standalone concept. It is woven into space. We find ourselves moving through time at different speeds as we move through space at different speeds. Einstein liked to talk of 'spacetime' in recognition of the fact that time works like a fourth dimension of space.

- **Nouns are actually verbs**: That is the real meaning of Einstein's famous equation: $E=mc^2$. Physicists might prefer to explain that E stands for energy while the m is mass and c is the speed of light. For the rest of the world, energy is about doing. It is action or the potential for action. It might be itself an abstract noun, but it is also what makes a verb a doing word. No energy: no doing. Mass is about stuff, physical substance: it is what things are made of. It represents the world of concrete nouns. Einstein's equation is saying that what we think of as things are really an expression of their potential to change. An illustration of this is the fact that a watch that has been wound up weighs a tiny amount more than a watch which has been left to run down. That is because some of its mass has been released in the form of kinetic energy (and perhaps a little heat). The reason we don't notice it is because the energy change is very small compared to c, the speed of light, which is the constant that Einstein suggested connected mass and energy.

- **Time and space are shaped by gravity**: This is the brain blender. We tend to think of gravity as a force of attraction that draws light things like apples to heavier things like planets. Einstein's biggest breakthrough was imagining gravity is created by shape, not attraction. This came to him as a result of what he later described as the happiest thought of his life: a man in free fall as a result of stepping off the top of a building. He imagined that such a person would not feel the effects of gravity. It sounds perverse. What he means is that if someone in that situation could shut out their thoughts of crashing to the ground, he or she would feel weightless. But what if instead of imagining gravity as a force pulling things down to the ground, we imagined it as the earth accelerating up towards us? Furthermore, what if that feeling that the earth is accelerating up towards us was not created by actual motion but by the shape of space and time getting distorted? We might not notice the acceleration if the dimensions of things and the timing of things were always changing to compensate. That is essentially what Einstein's theory of general relativity is. It is the idea that mass distorts the shape of spacetime.

It is important to get to grips with this concept because the shape of space and time is at the heart of Hawking's No Boundary Proposal. It helps eliminate boundaries at the Big Bang. The best way of understanding how shape rather that attraction causes gravity is to start by thinking what a straight line is. It is the shortest distance between two points. It also has a definition in Newton's first law of motion: a body travelling at a uniform speed will continue to travel in a straight line in unless a force acts on it.

We all know what a straight line looks like when drawn on a piece of paper, but when you try to draw one on a spherical planet like ours, you find that the shortest distance between two points is an arc. That is why when you are flying from London to New York your plane will travel much further north than it might do if were to plot a course with a ruler on a map. When Einstein says the shape of spacetime is distorted by mass, he means that it creates curved surfaces which curl the shortest distance between two points.

Let's go back to Einstein's man on the roof of a building. If there is no such thing as the force of gravity to bring him down, he just hangs in the air when he leaves the roof. If we think about this in terms of spacetime rather than just space, this means that he moves in a straight line in time, but not in space. Now let's turn gravity on. It starts distorting spacetime so that the rate at which time passes at the top of the building becomes a tiny bit faster than the rate at which time passes at the bottom of the building. This doesn't change what a straight line looks like in the three dimensions of space, but it does change what a straight line looks like in the four dimensions of spacetime. A straight line in spacetime involves the ground accelerating up to the man with a thud.

Gravity works in the same way at the planetary level. The mass of the sun distorts the shape of spacetime in the solar system to create elliptical orbits for the planets. Indeed, it was the study of the unusual orbit of Mercury, which could not be explained by conventional Newtonian physics, which ensured the rapid acceptance of Einstein's Theory of Relativity in scientific circles.

On a still bigger scale, imagine a situation where gravity is so strong that it not only shapes time. It stops time. That is what Hawking believes happens in black holes. It is also what he thinks happened at the Big Bang. The mass of the whole universe was compacted into something the size of a single atom of enormous density. The force of gravity was so extreme that it had the power to curve the time dimension to a standstill. It means that asking 'what happened before the Big Bang?' is a bit like asking what is south of the South Pole. There is no south after the South Pole. This is also part of what Hawking means by no boundaries. There is no necessary 'edge' which cannot be explained by physics. The beginning of time is smooth like a sphere.

However, Hawking's problem is that relativity on its own is not enough to explain the dynamics of the Big Bang. When all matter is squeezed together as densely as it was when time started, the physics of subatomic particles comes into play. That means quantum mechanics.

Quantum Mechanics: A Conspiracy Against Knowledge

Quantum mechanics boggles the mind in a different way from relativity. Gravity is part of our everyday experience of the world, but quantum mechanics is not. Its rules only apply to things much smaller that we can see. However, when one starts looking into this world, it confronts us with a weirdness that is impossible to comprehend. It challenges us to rethink the very meaning of knowledge. If quantum theory is right, even God doesn't know what is going on.

Let's start with the most basic question: what is the nature of matter? Is it made up of particles like discrete building blocks which take up space in a distinct location? Or is it made up of waves: disturbances in space which carry energy? In the 19th century the consensus was that the world was made up of both. Light came in waves but things with mass (such as atoms and molecules) came in particles. In the early 20th century, physicists learned to accept that things were a lot more complicated. A nice way of understanding this complication is through what is known as the double slit experiment.

The English polymath Thomas Young devised this experiment in 1801 to prove that light travelled in waves. He shone a beam of sunlight towards a screen via a panel with two slits cut in it. Instead of the light showing up on the screen as two distinct bands corresponding to the slits, it showed as a series of lines in what is known as an interference pattern. This is characteristic of waves, because when waves run into each other they either amplify each other or cancel each other out depending on how their peaks and troughs coincide.

When it later became possible to conduct the same experiment with individual particles (such as atoms and molecules) it became clear that they too behaved like waves. Fire off one particle through the slits and you get what you might expect: the particle you fired is detected as a discrete pinpoint on the screen (although its positioning might seem a bit random). Fire off another 100 particles and the randomness evaporates. Together the particles begin to build up the stripes of the interference pattern. It is as if each particle knows that it is supposed to be making a pattern with the other particles even before they are fired off.

Trying to spy on the particles as they make their journey between the gun and the screen doesn't help: there is an observer effect. That is because whatever you use to do the detection (for example sending in a beam of photons) interferes with the behaviour of the particles. If you put a detector in before or after the slits to watch the particles that you are trying to shoot at the screen, you don't get the interference pattern on the screen after firing off 100 particles. You get two bands of particles detected on the screen corresponding to the position of the two slits.

It seems as if particles behave in one way when they are being observed, and another when they are not.

Most normal people would run screaming from the lab vowing never to look at a particle ever again after being confronted with this behaviour. How is it that these tiny critters that make up the basic building blocks of the universe can behave so self-consciously?

Physicists seem a more phlegmatic breed. Over the past century or so, they have built a whole new area of physics — quantum mechanics — around the implausibility of particle behaviour. This includes the following concepts:

- **There are absolute limits to what we can know:** At the heart of quantum physics is the fact that we can't know both the position and speed of a particle (such as a photon, electron, atom or molecule) with perfect accuracy. The more we try to nail down its position, the less we can know about the speed and vice versa. This isn't because our measuring equipment isn't good enough or because we don't quite understand the physics. It seems to be a fact that we have to accept about the world.

- **A new way of understanding existence:** In quantum physics you can't say with any certainty what exists. That is because the act of observation seems to crystalise a shard of reality but not the complete picture. Unobserved particles behave like waves: they have no specific location or energy level. They could be anywhere doing anything. It is a bit like a game of grandmother's footsteps. As soon as you look round to see what they are up to they stop being waves and behave like particles again, assuming a specific location and energy level. There is no rhyme or reason behind the specific location. The best you can do is assign a probability to each possibility of where a particle might be. This means that instead of thinking of unobserved particles as waves, we can think of them as functions of probability and then we can start getting maths to work on them. This approach has given quantum physics extraordinarily accurate powers of prediction and made inventions such as lasers, MRI scanners, and electron microscopes possible.

- **History contains every possibility:** In quantum physics when a particle goes from A to B, we have to assume that it travels on every single possible path from A to B. It means that there is no single history of that journey. Instead, physicists use the sum over all possible histories when they need an equation or expression to refer to the path of a particle. Conceptually it is a difficult assumption to get one's mind around: our experience of history is that there is one path, not multiple paths to the present. However, it works well mathematically. The 'sum over histories' approach appears to be the best way of predicting the allowable orbits of atoms and molecules.

- **An unintelligent design:** Hawking believed that quantum mechanics holds the key to the No Boundary Proposal. There is no single moment of creation in a quantum world. Instead, every possible moment of creation is assumed to have happened. That is because with the whole of existence squeezed up into the size of a single atom the rules of quantum mechanics apply to space and time as well as particles. In one of those possible moments of creation, time could have separated from space and led to the expansion of our universe in a Big Bang. It means that our creator, God, could be replaced by the randomness of quantum behaviour.

Hawking does not go further into the implications of this in *A Brief History of Time*. Instead, he focuses on the different theories which might enable quantum theory to accommodate relativity's understanding of gravity.

This idea of multiple possible moments of creation does however leave one big question hanging in the air. What happened to all the other parallel universes spawned by all the other moments of creation predicted by quantum mechanics? Hawking made this the subject of his subsequent book (written with Leonard Mlodinow) *The Grand Design*. In it he discusses how, in the beginning, different parallel universes might have arisen in 'quantum bubbles', each subject to different physical constants. Most of these would have collapsed immediately, but a minority — perhaps 10^{500} (ie 10 with 500 zeros after it) would have been robust enough to survive. Our universe would be one of those persistent universes which also in one region of it supports the possibility of life.[71]

This explanation also addresses another argument for the existence of God: the argument by design. This is the idea that the existence of a universe which can support life is so extraordinarily unlikely that it must have been set up deliberately. Hawking's answer undercuts the title of his book. There is no grand design. The habitability of our universe is probable for two reasons. Firstly, because if there are such a huge number of universes which are robust enough to survive, the idea that there is one small region of one universe which might support life doesn't look so improbable. Secondly, because if we are here to observe the universe, we should not be surprised that we exist in that part of a particular universe that supports life.

According to his graduate student, Thomas Hertog, Hawking was still developing this theory in the years before his death in 2018. Hertog published these ideas in a book entitled *On the Origin of Time: Stephen Hawking's Last Theory* in 2023. The title is supposed to resonate with the title of Darwin's great work *On the Origin of the Species*. That is because it introduces an evolutionary element to the understanding of the beginning of time.

Its central thesis is that the universe has not one history but every possible history, but as we look backwards into it towards the beginning of time our act of observation crystalises these probabilities into a single path.

It means that we can imagine that the universe did not have a defined set of initial laws. Instead, the physical laws which we now know govern the universe could have evolved through a process of natural selection. The random possibilities of quantum mechanics provide the variation: the enormous number of possible permutations and combinations of physical constants which might define different universes. Our being here to observe the outcome (and thereby collapse the wave function in quantum terms) would have provided the process of selection. It is a coherent hypothesis which might seem to leave little room for a God to programme the initial laws of the universe so that they support life.

It doesn't represent the final nail in God's coffin, however.

In *On the Origin of Time*, Hertog points out that Hawking was not the first person to see the potential for an evolutionary model of the universe driven by quantum mechanics interacting with the theory of relativity. That honour goes to a Belgian priest named Georges Lemaître (1894–1966). In 1931, Lemaître wrote a 457-word letter to the scientific journal, *Nature*, where he explained what became the kernel of Hawking's No Boundary Proposal:

'If the world has begun with a single quantum, the notions of space and time would altogether fail to have any meaning at the beginning; they would only begin to have a sensible meaning when the original quantum had been divided into a sufficient number of quanta. If this suggestion is correct, the beginning of the world happened a little before the beginning of space and time.'[72]

Lemaître was not concerned that this point of view might set him up against God or the Church. He believed that science and religion could coexist and complement each other, with science exploring the natural world through empirical investigation and religion addressing questions of meaning, purpose, and the ultimate nature of reality. 'There is no conflict between religion and science,' he said. 'They are both seeking the same truth, just in different ways.'

Sidebar: What Exists?

Quantum mechanics works well mathematically, but it doesn't work well conceptually. What does it mean to say everything is a probability until it is observed? Our experience of the world is concrete and our experience of history is fixed. The physicist, Carlo Rovelli, has proposed an alternative way of understanding it. We should assume that the only thing that exists is interactions; not things or particles or waves or even probabilities.

'A thing is something which remains equal to itself. A stone is a thing because I can ask where the stone is tomorrow, while a happening is something that is limited in space and time. A kiss is not a thing, because I cannot ask, where is a kiss, tomorrow; "Where is this kiss?" tomorrow. I mean, it's just happened now. And I think that we don't understand the world as made by stones, by things. We understand the world made by kisses, or things like kisses — happenings.'[73]

Where Is God in Stephen Hawking's Brief History of Time?

Three big questions about God seem to fall out of *A Brief History of Time*:

1. What if we don't need God to explain the beginning of things?
2. Can we keep God and science in separate boxes?
3. How does any of this relate to us on a personal level?

I used them to set the agenda for the youth discussion group at the University Church, and I will use this section to record that discussion.

The group seemed engaged as I explained what *A Brief History of Time* was about: the idea of quantum physics certainly captured their imagination. We got waylaid in a discussion of whether Toy Story or Instagram was a better analogy for the behaviour of unobserved particles. In Toy Story the toys only come alive when there are no adults looking. On Instagram we never get to see the chaos of people's lives between their perfect posts.

Just to make sure everyone has grasped what Hawking is trying to say, I offered the following summary of his book:

'There are two important ideas in physics: one explains big things like stars and planets; and the other explains tiny things like atoms. The first idea, called relativity, says that gravity can make time slow down and even stop. The second idea, called quantum mechanics, says that tiny particles can do all sorts of surprising and unpredictable things. When the universe began with the Big Bang, both big and small things were squashed together, so both relativity and quantum mechanics were at work. Everything including time could have come from randomness and nothingness. We don't necessarily need God as a creator.'

Creation without a Creator

I start off by asking Marion, who seems to have been most attentive, what she thinks this means for God.

'It all went above my head a bit,' she confesses. 'I can see that there might be a scientific explanation of how the world began, but I am not sure that the mechanism is important. I was then trying to think what was important.'

And what did you come up with?

'I am not sure. Is it existence? When we say God made the world, aren't we really saying God caused existence to exist?'

'That's heavy,' remarks James. 'So does that mean that God had to wait until existence existed, before He could exist.'

'Don't be silly,' Marion says before her sister Freya joins the conversation.

'Maybe God made Himself exist before existence existed,' she suggests, not entirely helpfully.

'Or maybe God made existence exist retroactively so he could exist to make existence exist,' James adds. I am worried that I am losing control of the conversation, but Marion continues unperturbed.

'That's the problem, I think. I don't think anyone really knows what they are talking about with this stuff. It all ends up sounding like nonsense.'

I ask George if he can help us.

'I see what you are saying, but I don't think it is just a problem with religious language. I have actually read *A Brief History of Time*. Some of the things it suggests seem to make sense in terms of maths but I just can't get my head around what they mean in real life. This quantum stuff is mind-bending.'

'But it works,' George's brother, Harry puts in. 'None of those inventions like lasers and electron microscopes would exist without it.'

'So you are saying that a Sony PlayStation disproves the existence of God?' George replies sardonically.

'It does sort of,' Harry asserts. 'It means that quantum physics works, and if quantum physics works, it could explain how the universe began. Where does that leave God?'

'What I am trying to say is that it is not clear to me what the actual meaning of it all is,' George replies patiently.

'So does that mean that "physics does me 'ead in!" is now a proof of the existence of God.' Harry suggests to get his own back on George.

'No. That's not what I am saying. I am agreeing with Marion I think. I think if a religious person says that "God is the basis of existence", it is not clear whether that statement is contradicted by the statement: "unified field theory can explain the beginning of the universe without the need for an external actor to set the boundary conditions". It is a question of language rather than science.'

I then turn to James to see whether he is convinced by this argument.

'I think religious people never want to be convinced of anything different from what they believe. They use slippery language to avoid it.'

I say that I think that everyone's language becomes pretty slippery when we are talking about things which are so remote from our experience.

'Well what do you think of what Hawking says about there being no time or space for God to exist in before the Big Bang?' James asks.

I say that I am not sure. God is supposed to be beyond time and space. It shouldn't matter.

James responds with another difficult question. 'This is what I wonder about. Whenever anyone talks about God they just say He is the most you can be in everything you can think of. Time, space, strength, cleverness, speed. He has the most everything-ness. Don't you think it also means He also has the most nothing-ness?'

I say that the problem is that God is supposed to be beyond human conception so we should expect words to be inadequate.

Here Harry joins in again. 'That sounds like a convenient excuse.'

I say it is not an easy issue to resolve, and then bring Rosamond into the conversation. She has been quiet so far. What does she think of all this?

'I'm worried. I am going to university next year to study science and none of these scientists believe in God. I think I might be the same.'

She is talking honestly. I ask her what specific things she is worried about. She says doesn't know.

I remind her of the story of Lemaître: how he was one of the pioneers of relativity and quantum physics but remained a priest until his death. It seems a good moment to move onto the next topic.

Separate Boxes for God and Science

I start by summing up the conversation so far. We have been flailing around in the mud. The central problem is not the relationship between science and religion, it is the relationship between language and science. Science doesn't really recognise statements like 'God is the basis for existence' or 'God is beyond time'. They have too many possible meanings, many of them completely unfathomable. It means that they can't be stated in a scientific way that can either be proved or disproved. Does this mean that we can keep science and religion in completely separate boxes?

Rosamond picks up the challenge. 'I don't think it really works. That Belgian priest might have been able to do it, but I don't think that Hawking would have agreed with him. That's the whole idea of the No Boundary Proposal. There are no boundaries. That means you can't separate science off from everything else.'

I say I think that Hawking was talking specifically about there being no boundary conditions for the maths behind the workings of the universe.

'But when you are talking about the universe, you are talking about everything in it. Not just the maths of it. Where do you think the boundary between science and the rest is?'

I try to compose an answer. I am not sure I have a good one. Fortunately, I am rescued by a question from Freya, Marion's precocious younger sister.

'Do you think God also has no boundaries?'

Yes, of course.

'So if God has no boundaries how can God be in a different box to science?'

James joins in here. 'That sounds like another thing to add to God's list of everything-ness. He's got no boundaries, and even more nothing-ness.'

'You are saying He, rather than She. That is also a boundary,' Marion adds.

And vice versa I add. Perhaps it boils down to a battle of the boundaries. Should a No Boundary God obey the laws of physics?

The consensus is not. Why would He make such laws then?

'He made them for us, because otherwise the world wouldn't work,' Freya suggests.

So would God be a physical thing? Nobody is sure of this. They can see the problem. If God is a physical thing He or She should be detectable by physics. If He or She is not a physical thing in any way, then He or She has a boundary.

'I suppose that is where Jesus comes in. He was the physical bit of God,' George suggests.

He doesn't seem very convinced. I push him on it.

'I don't think it would convince Hawking. Why would God only have a physical presence for such as short space of time so long ago. I am sure Hawking would see that as another boundary.' George concedes.

Rosamond is now getting excited. She takes a page from my notes and my pen, and announces that she knows how God can have no boundaries between the physical and the non-physical.

She writes on the paper the following equation:

God ≥ The Universe

What does that mean?

'It means that I think that if God has no boundaries, then He or She has to be the whole physical universe as well as anything else that might be out there, spiritual, abstract or whatever. It cuts out the whole problem of God and science being in separate boxes. They are in the same box. Come on, tell me I am clever!'

I am impressed. It aligns very much with my own thinking. The others are not sure what to make of it.

'So you think this table is part of God?' Freya asks.

'Why not?'

'It doesn't look very clean,' Freya points out.

'It makes a lot more sense than James' list of God's everything-nesses. Why not just say that God is everything?'

'Because it is not in the Bible,' says Harry. 'Isn't it called pantheism when you say God is in everything?'

Here George introduces his theological knowledge to the conversation.

'I think strictly speaking Pantheism would be saying that God is equal to the physical universe and nothing more. What Rosamond is talking about is called "panentheism". That is where God is in the universe but beyond that as well. I assume that is what you meant with the greater than or equals sign.'

'I suppose I did. I thought I was being clever thinking of it.' Rosamond is a bit crestfallen. 'Is it OK to be a panentheist? And a Christian I mean?'

I say that it really doesn't matter how you conceive of God because it is always bound to be wrong. He or She is supposed to be beyond conception.

'So is it OK if I worship this table?' Freya asks.

I say that I think the idea of Christianity is that we relate to God through the person of Jesus and it is a bit difficult to see how the table might relate to Jesus.

'Knowing you Freya, I am surprised you haven't started worshipping the loo,' Marion adds in a sisterly way.

Here Rowan joins the conversation. 'What did Stephen Hawking think about Jesus?' she asks.

This question catches me unawares. It is difficult to make the leap from big picture cosmology and the creation of the world to the person of Jesus. I say that I didn't think he was bothered by Jesus because he didn't think God existed.

'Hmm,' he says. 'You just said it didn't matter how we imagined God because Jesus is more important, but then you are saying that if you don't get God right you won't bother with Jesus.'

That is not quite what I said, but I can see where he is coming from. God is supposed to be both personal and universal. For Christianity to work, people have to believe in both. It seems a good moment to move on to our final question.

A Universal but Personal God

I start with Rosamond. How does she think her equation God $\geq$ The Universe might relate to her on a personal level. I immediately see that it is too direct a question: she really doesn't want to offer an answer — she has exposed her thoughts enough for the day. I wonder about asking George, but fear we might be in for a lecture. Marion seems to be avoiding my gaze.

I say it is a difficult thing. It is easy to talk about God on a philosophical level, but our thoughts on our relationship with God on a personal level are usually much too fragile to expose.

Harry contests this. 'Maybe that is because they sound so ridiculous when you say them aloud.'

Maybe it is, I agree.

'Maybe they are ridiculous,' Harry adds.

I don't think this approach to the discussion is going to get anyone to open up, so I try a different way into the subject.

What does the group think it would take to make Stephen Hawking believe in Jesus?

Freya has an immediate answer. 'If he made him better.'

I hadn't expected this. What does she mean?

'If Jesus made him better so he didn't have to use his wheelchair anymore and could talk normally and could do lots of maths on his own.'

How would that work I ask?

'He would pray to Jesus and Jesus would heal him?'

I am in a quandary here. I don't like to be seen squashing young people's beliefs, but at the same time I want to steer people away from believing prayer works like that. So I ask a different question.

How do you think the world would be different if God had cured Stephen Hawking's motor neurone disease?

'Everyone would think it was a miracle and believe in God as well,' Freya replies brightly. I seem to be digging myself deeper into a hole.

What about the other people who had motor neurone disease?

'God could also cure them.'

And all the other pain and suffering in the world? What about death?

'If everyone did what God wanted, he would make everything good.'

Here Harry's scepticism comes to the rescue. 'So why doesn't he then?' he asks.

Freya suddenly loses her confidence and looks to me for an answer.

I say, let's imagine what the world would be like if God did just fix everything for us. What would be the point of being human?

Freya perks up a bit at this question. 'So that we do what God wants,' she replies.

But would you have any choice in doing what God wants?

Freya is unsure. George takes over.

'I think what you are trying to say is that if God reliably answered everyone's prayers, we would lose an element of free will. There would be no point in doing bad things because you would always be better off obeying God and getting exactly what you want.'

Yes, I say, pointing out that there is a nice paradox in that. Part of our definition of being good is being selfless, but in this world being selfless would have no meaning. You could pray to God to make everyone rich and healthy and live for ever and it would happen at no real cost to yourself.

I can see that Harry doesn't like where the conversation is going. I ask him what he thinks.

'What you seem to be saying is that it would be ridiculous to expect God to respond to prayers directly, but you are not really coming up with a better answer idea of how this personal God might work.'

George steps in to defend me. 'Of course he isn't. This is called the problem of evil: how can a good God let bad things happen? There is no solution.'

I say that I will try to come up with something that works.

Let's go back to the Garden of Eden, I say. That is the equivalent of Freya's world where God does everything for us. To be human we need free will. We need to be able to choose between good and evil. This brings suffering into the world because once we can choose evil, bad things start happening in the world. Outside Eden we can't talk to God like Adam and Eve talked to God. Instead, we are left with this mysterious sense that God is still there and our duty is to understand God's will. Furthermore, the more that we sense that this is important, the more important it becomes to us. That is what a personal God means to me, I explain.

Harry is unconvinced: 'It still doesn't explain why God gave Stephen Hawking motor neurone disease.'

I guess that it doesn't. Maybe that is where the idea of God being in the world comes in. If we think of God as being this extraordinary flourishing thing that is life, it makes it easier to accept that everything including cancer and motor neurone disease might have a role to play.

'But what is the point of God if he won't actually change things for you.'

I say that there are two answers to that. The first is that trying to understand the purposes of God is probably what we are here for. The second is that when life is really terrible there is a consolation in knowing that your life is bound together into something much bigger — this creative force of the universe —

that cares about you, and whose care you feel more the more that you care about it.

James sees the irony in all of this. 'You seem to be saying that Stephen Hawking should have forgotten the Big Bang and gone back to Genesis.'

I say that *A Brief History of Time* is one story about how God works in the world. Genesis is another. Both are important and entirely compatible. It is time to end the session.

Conclusion

So where is God? That was the question I promised to answer in this chapter. The answer I am offering here is that God is in the world, or more precisely God is greater than or equal to the universe. Obviously, God remains beyond our conception. This idea of God is just a placeholder formulation, like the old man with a beard in the sky. We can use it if we find ourselves having to think about the nature of God, without feeling that it is the final definition of God. But as a placeholder it solves two big problems that are faced by Christianity in particular, as well as by religion in general.

The first is the relationship with the physical world of science. In this formulation there is nothing that you can learn about the world that doesn't tell you more about God. God is the world. Science is the study of God — without boundaries. Nobody needs to tiptoe around each new breakthrough in particle physics or cell biology worrying that it might squeeze God out of the last remaining gaps in our knowledge. We need to think of science as the author Philip Pullman did in his Northern Lights trilogy: it is applied theology.

From my perspective, teaching young people in the Old Library of Oxford's University Church, it is a return to the original purpose of the University: to bring us to a better understanding of God. It brings to mind the motto of the university: *Dominus Illuminatio Mea* — the Lord enlightens me.

The second problem this 'God in the world' idea solves is how we can have a personal relationship with this enormous and abstract thing called God? The advantage of the 'old man in the sky' placeholder for God was that it enabled us to think about God as a supportive parent who listened to us and sympathised with us. We could have a personal relationship with him. The idea that we are all children of God is still a useful way of understanding God, but 'the old man in the sky' has become intellectually difficult to sustain as the main way we picture God in our minds. Over the past 300 years philosophy, science and even feminism, have pushed us to understand God in a steadily more abstract direction. We have piled on the superlatives: omniscient, all-powerful, beyond space and time — while at the same time steadily withdrawing God's physical presence from the world. This idea that we, together with the whole physical world, are part of God, reverses that trend. It enables us to understand our relationship with God as being both concrete and absolutely intimate.

Perhaps the relationship is different from the parent-child analogy that we get from the God as an 'old man in the sky placeholder', but it has other Biblical parallels. In 2 Corinthians Chapter 12 verses 12–27 St Paul suggests that we as individuals are like the individual parts of the body, which together make up the whole. We need to live our lives as if we are part of this whole. This message lies at the heart of the Communion prayer: 'Although we are many, we are one body,' we say.

What I am trying to say here is that Panentheism — the idea that the universe is an emanation of God — is not a fringe heresy. It is a way of understanding the relationship between God and the world which is wholly in keeping with scripture (although like every other placeholder or metaphor for God, it is not a definitive one).

For myself I like to embroider ideas around this concept. Could we, for example, think of God as the consciousness of the universe? Consciousness is a strange thing. It seems to grow out of the interaction of the disparate parts of the brain without itself having a single 'seat' or organ which does the job of making us conscious. Maybe God is like that. We are like his synaptic brain cells each going about our business but between us creating this intelligence that unites us all.

This body and the members analogy underscores the importance of the commandments to love God and love our neighbour. Loving God means loving the whole of creation. This love is what makes God flourish. The commandment to love our neighbour is part of that too, but it challenges us to ask: 'who is our neighbour?' Isn't every living creature our neighbour?

This line of thinking brings Christianity back into line with mainstream spirituality. My view is that the majority of people still feel that life offers something elusive that is more than meets the eye. They can't easily define it, but nor can they easily reject it. In the past this is what led people towards religion. Over the past 30 years, however, religion's lack of leadership on the environmental crisis together with its obsession with social conservatism, has meant that conventional religions no longer speak to this sense.

This thought sets us up nicely for the next and final chapter: a discussion of Richard Dawkins' atheist blockbuster, *The God Delusion*. The great geneticist would probably have little argument with what has been written in this book so far, but he would point out there are still some big obstacles to be crossed before we reach an understanding of a benign and believable God — namely, the fact that the Christian God is vengeful in his judgement. He sends bad people to hell and good people to heaven. He defies science with miracles and raises people from the dead. It is dangerous nonsense that creates misery in the world.

Chapter 5

Richard Dawkins: *The Selfish Gene*

What Is Faith?

Introduction

Here is the challenge. Richard Dawkins wrote *The God Delusion* with the object of creating more atheists. In the introduction to the book, he wrote: 'If this book works as I intend, religious readers who open it will be atheists when they put it down.' My objective in this chapter is to explain how Dawkins' book might be read to have the reverse effect. An atheist might be able to pick up *The God Delusion*, and by the time they put it down they have come to believe in God. But that is not all. I think that they should also be able to agree with most of what Dawkins[74] has to say.

The first three chapters of this book may have taken us three quarters of the way towards this goal. Our discussion of Nietzsche, Derrida and Hawking addresses three of Dawkins' objections to religion.

The central thesis of *The God Delusion* is that religion is not just nonsense, but dangerous nonsense. It should not be tolerated in public any longer. Writing in the wake of the 9/11 attacks in New York and Washington, this argument struck a chord with many readers. In the chapter on Nietzsche's *Thus Spoke Zarathustra* we discussed how the evils of religion seem to grow out of our very human will to power. The conclusion we reached was that if Christians want to live like Christ, we need to reject our instinct for power in favour of love. If we can do this, then we can distance ourselves from 90 per cent of the abuses of religion — from the Crusades to today's culture wars.

Much of Dawkins' anger against religion is directed against those who believe in the literal truth of the Bible. As an evolutionary biologist, he is particularly opposed to creationists who reject Darwin's theory of evolution. We addressed this issue in the chapter on Jacques Derrida's *Writing and Difference*. Derrida's post-structuralism forces us to confront the fact that there can be no ultimate truth in scripture. Such is the nature of language. It need not make religion impossible, however. It means that the act of belief is a pursuit. We pursue God through infinite layers of meaning, both in scripture and in the world. We should not expect to reach a conclusion. Instead, we should find holiness in the journey.

Of course, Dawkins' main point in *The God Delusion* is that God is a delusion. He or She does not exist in any meaningful way, and those who believe are deluded. His main argument against God is a scientific one. If science can reliably explain everything, then the only point of God is to provide us with an imaginary friend. With so much scientific evidence now suggesting that God does not exist, it is time to grow up and wave goodbye to this imaginary friend. We talked about the challenge of resolving science and religion in the chapter on Stephen Hawking's *A Brief History of Time*. The conclusion we reached was that we need to accept that God *is* creation. This 'no boundary' hypothesis means that all science is an investigation of God. It can coexist with religion without conflict. In that sense Dawkins' research on the genetics of evolution becomes an exploration of God's workings in the world, rather than a contradiction of them.

None of these three arguments directly contradict Dawkins. We all agree that religion does bad things (but it doesn't have to). We can also agree that there is a lot of nonsense in scripture if you try to read it too literally. There is no dispute with Dawkins on the origin of humanity if we understand the evolution of the natural world as an emanation of God. Nevertheless, there is still one big issue that stands between Dawkins and God. It is faith.

I don't think it is possible to get Dawkins across that obstacle. I don't think that faith comes from clever arguments. What I think I can offer is a different understanding of the nature of faith. I think *The God Delusion* gives some good insight into that, and I hope that when readers have a better idea of the size and shape of the obstacle they face, they might be able to find their own way through it to God. That is why I am going to make finding an answer to the question: 'what is faith?' the objective of this chapter.

Sidebar: Atheism and Nihilism

Some say Richard Dawkins is an amateur atheist. He might not believe in God but he does have values in which he believes. For example, the importance he attaches to objective truth, to beauty, to goodness, and to the progress of humanity does not arise from reason alone. A nihilist would argue that this arises from an irrational sentimentality about life and the future.

The best place to start if you want to understand this point of view is *Straw Dogs* by the anti-humanist philosopher, John Gray. It was the first book I introduced to the youth discussion group at the University Church. It is so bleak in its assessment of the human condition that it will make you want to believe in anything. The basic thesis of the book is that humanity is pointless and transient. As a species we cannot bear this truth and make up all kinds of stories to convince ourselves that it might be otherwise. The 'straw dogs' of the title are the offerings to the gods used in ancient Chinese rituals. 'During the ritual they were treated with utmost reverence', Gray explains. 'When it was over and they were no longer needed they were trampled on and tossed aside.'[75]

Gray has little time for Dawkins' belief in science and the progress of humanity. These are also pathetic stories we tell ourselves to avoid the dismal truth. Gray attacks Dawkins' atheism directly in his subsequent book, *Seven Types of Atheism* (another favourite of our discussion group). The premise of this book is that there are many sects within atheism, just as there are many sects within religion. Gray investigates the validity of seven of them:

The New Atheism: The belief that science should dispel religion — he suggests Dawkins is this kind of atheist. Gray thinks it is flawed because science is not a world view. It is a method of inquiry — a tool that the human animal has invented to deal with a world it cannot fully understand. 'The very idea that we live in a law-governed cosmos may be not much more than a fading legacy of faith in a divine lawgiver,'[76] Gray remarks.

Secular humanism: The belief in human progress making a better world over time. Gray thinks that this is simply wrong. Technology may improve but humanity doesn't. He lists John Stuart Mill, Karl Marx, Bertrand Russell and Ayn Rand as secular humanists. 'Without exception these atheists have been convinced they were promoting the cause of humanity. In every case, the species whose progress they believed they were advancing was a phantom of their imagination.'[77]

A religion of science: this is the belief that humans can use technology to transcend the physical world. Gray sees this in a number of scientific fads from the formation of genetic super-races to the use of bio-engineering and artificial intelligence to enhance the powers of humanity. Unlike Yuval Noah Harari, author of *Homo Deus: A Brief History of Tomorrow*, Gray does not see this process ending with the creation of a God-like race. Humanity will retain its intractable enmities and divisions, and the best we can hope for is to become 'a warring pantheon of gods'[78] like those imagined by Homer.

Political religions: political change can bring heaven to earth. From the Dominion of Munster in sixteenth-century Germany to French Jacobinism and the Russian Revolution, the rulers of these utopias often turn out to have a remarkable thirst for blood. The creed of liberalism does not escape Gray's censure, highlighting the bloodshed in Iraq and Afghanistan that grew out of the belief in the heavenly qualities of liberal democracy. There is no political nirvana.

The God haters: this kind of atheism grows out of the problem of evil; if God is all powerful, and all good, then how can He allow bad things to happen? The conclusion is that God must be evil and should be hated out of existence. The contradiction in this is obvious: 'If you look beyond Christian and anti-Christian polemic, you do not need to invoke religion to explain cruelty. Like kindness it goes with being human,'[79] Gray explains.

Atheism without progress: there is no God, but no piety towards humanity either. Joseph Conrad, the Polish-born author who spent most of his early life at sea, is an example of this kind of atheist. 'The seamen's struggle with the ocean is a cipher for the human situation in a godless universe,' Gray writes. Conrad found the mechanical process in which humans are caught tragic. None of the visions of improvement conjured up by modern thinkers could stand up against his 'deep-seated sense of fatality governing this man-inhabited world'. But it was this invincible fatality that evoked the qualities he found most worthwhile in human beings.[80] Gray warms to the idea of atheism without progress.

The atheism of silence: this is a paradoxical kind of atheism, where God exists but is so quiet that He or She might as well not exist. The most famous exponent of it was the Jewish philosopher, Baruch Spinoza (1632–1677). He believed that God is in the world, but this world is self-subsistent. As Gray explains: 'The world is a universal system in which everything is as it must be. Nothing is contingent, and there are no miracles. In such a world the only possible freedom is freedom of mind, which means understanding that things cannot be other than they are.'[81]

From a philosophical point of view, Dawkins' belief in science cannot be said to be wholly rational. As Nietzsche pointed out: 'Science too rests on a faith; there is no science "without presuppositions"'.[82] The proofs of science rely on science to become proofs. The German philosopher also argued that once God was dead, we can only understand the world through our own consciousness. Truth and values become objects of our own creation.

It raises the question: what is the qualitative difference between belief in God and belief in science, progress, and humanity?

Where Is He Coming From?

I will break this section into three parts. The first will look at how the perspective of Dawkins' age might have informed his thinking. His assumption that religion still has a powerful grip on the West seems anachronistic, but it also sheds some light on how we might understand the meaning of faith. The second section will look at his background as an evolutionary biologist by looking at the ideas that grow out of his 1976 book, *The Selfish Gene*. The final section will, in the spirit of provocation, show how the same mathematical theory that underpins *The Selfish Gene* can be used to explain the resilience of the God meme.

Another Country

Dawkins was born in Nairobi, Kenya, in 1941. The family subsequently moved to Malawi, but returned to England in 1949. His age means that he represents the last generation of Britons who grew up with the expectation that they would be Christian. It shapes the premise of *The God Delusion*. Much of the energy of the book comes from the idea that children are being brainwashed by their parents into becoming Christians. Dawkins wants the book to be a liberation for these people.

The God Delusion begins with an anecdote about how Dawkins' wife, Lalla, was miserable at school and wanted to leave. She never told her parents until years later when her mother was aghast: 'But darling, why didn't you come and tell us?' she reportedly asked. 'I didn't know I could,' Lalla replied. Dawkins then makes this his 'text for today'.

'I suspect — well, I am sure — that there are lots of people out there who have been brought up in some religion or other, are unhappy in it, don't believe it, or are worried about the evils that are done in its name; people who feel vague yearnings to leave their parents religion and wish they could, but just don't realise that leaving is an option. If you are one of them this book is for you.'

The God Delusion gives the impression that religion is a vast, maximum-security prison controlled by cruel and determined fanatics, who ensure complete adherence to its rules. Dawkins sees himself as one of the few free thinkers who has escaped, and it is his duty to help others break free.

Yet that is not a world most of us would recognise today. When Dawkins was 10 years old in 1951, 86 per cent[83] of Britons identified as Christian. That figure had fallen to 46 per cent[84] in 2021, with 37 per cent declaring that they belonged to no religion at all. On average, fewer than 3 per cent of the population of the UK attend church regularly.[85] Mosque attendance overtook Church of England attendance in Britain in 2004.[86] The US appears more Christian and more religious, but it is following a similar path. The Pew Research Centre predicts that by 2070 Christians will almost certainly be in a minority in America. The biggest driver of this trend is the decline of the so-called 'seven sisters' of American Protestantism.[87] These churches saw their combined membership fall from 62.4 million people in 1960 to 16.0 million in 2018.[88] Some of this decline has been related to splits over attitudes to gay and lesbian issues, but death and defection explain most of it. According to the Pew Research Centre only 45 per cent of those who grow up in one of these seven mainline denominations remain with it later in life.

Evangelical Churches (which anachronistically are not considered to be part of the traditional protestant mainstream) have not been immune from these trends. The largest evangelical grouping in the US, the Southern Baptist Convention, saw its membership fall from 16.0 million in 2000 to 13.2 million in 2022.[89]

The Catholic Church has fared better than Protestantism in both the UK and US, largely because of immigration (from Eastern Europe in the UK, and from Latin America in the US), but it has also suffered a massive outflow of members. In 2021 there were 30.1 million adults in the US who claimed to be 'former Catholics' compared with 3.5 million in 1970.[90]

It makes Dawkins' idea that there are a huge number of believers who 'didn't know I could' leave the church look deeply outdated. Even when he was writing *The God Delusion* in the mid-2000s, any Christian would have to be remarkably unobservant not to notice that people were slipping away from the pews.

This is perhaps where my notional atheist picking up their copy of *The God Delusion* might start reading the possibility of faith in his text. It is difficult to see Christianity today as a penal institution from which only a few independent thinkers have broken free. Atheism has become the ideology of the cultural establishment in the UK and in large parts of the United States. It has locked the minds of a generation against faith. To be a believer today — in the UK and the big coastal cities of the US — is to be a rebel against the status quo.

And yet there are some parts of Christianity in Europe and North America[91] where Dawkins' vision of young people trapped in faiths in which they do not believe may be true. Some Churches are growing rapidly and seem to exert an extraordinary hold over their congregations. For example, membership of non-denominational evangelical megachurches rose by 10 per cent to 21 million between 2010 and 2020.[92] Typically, these Churches are run by captivating preachers who attract congregations of tens of thousands on Sundays and reach a still larger broadcast audience. Some older denominations are also thriving. Assemblies of God was founded in 1914, but it saw membership grow from 2.6 million in 2000 to 3.3 million in 2020. It is a pentecostalist Church with the emphasis on speaking in tongues, healing, and prophecy. Even the Amish, an anabaptist sect brought to Pennsylvania in the early eighteenth century, and now famous for buggies and bonnets, is piling on new members. Its numbers grew from 178,000 in 2000 to 373,000 in 2022. Mormonism has also been phenomenally successful. Its membership rose from 12.9 million in 2006 — the year that *The God Delusion* was published — to 17.0 million in 2022[93] (although its growth rate has markedly slowed in recent years).

What these 'successful' churches seem to have in common is the strength they get from rejecting the mores of the world; and the social and emotional commitment they expect from their members. It means that for many young people brought up in these Churches, it is genuinely difficult to leave. They worry about being cut off from friends and family. They are more fearful of the secular world. They may also have been required to make public and emotionally sincere commitments to their beliefs (for example in recounting the intimate moment of their rebirth in Christ) which may be difficult to renounce.

It also raises the question: what is faith? Is it in the numbers, with growing Churches showing stronger faith than shrinking ones? Is it in buggies and bonnets? Is it in the rejection science? Or in the ostracism of friends and relatives? Are all these things faith? Or are they just the performance of faith?

I think most people would agree that faith is a private matter between God and themselves. However, in a way it is like quantum mechanics. Once observed, it becomes something else. It becomes part of the performance. We all want to look like good Christians.

It is difficult for an atheist like Dawkins to see this performative aspect of religion. Without being open to the sense of God, he can't be expected to know how difficult it might be for people to think candidly about their sense of God. That is, in part, because the language isn't there to express the transcendent. Instead we have adopted ceremonies and ritualised language that we feel touch on it in some way. More mundanely, it also because there is pressure to say what you think those around you want to hear.

Dawkins has a soft spot for Anglican traditions and culture. A fellow of New College in Oxford, he enjoys what he describes as the 'magical' choral music that the college's ancient endowment affords. Founded in 1379 by William of Wykeham, then Bishop of Winchester, as 'great chantry to make intercession for the repose of his soul' the college is a performance of medieval faith that has lasted nearly six and a half centuries.

At the University Church we too have a magical choir and carved medieval stonework. We have Newman's pulpit, embroidered vestments and a ceiling painted with the constellation of Cassiopeia. This is how we perform our religion. Others perform it by professing to be saved, speaking in tongues, and, yes, condemning homosexuals and burning evolutionist school books. This is the show of faith. It is the earthquake, wind and fire. It is not faith itself.

Richard Dawkins became an atheist when he was a child for much the same reason that Friedrich Nietzsche did. He couldn't see why he should choose Christianity as his religion simply because that was the religion of his parents. He explains his choice in his 2019 book *Outgrowing God*.

'I went to Christian schools and was confirmed in the Church of England when I was 13. I finally gave up Christianity when I was 15. One of the reasons why gave it up was this. I had already worked out when I was about nine that if I had been born to Viking parents, I would have firmly believed in Odin and Thor. If I had been born in ancient Greece I would worship Zeus and Aphrodite. In modern times if I had been born in Pakistan or Egypt, I would believe that Jesus was only a prophet, not the son of God as the Christian priests teach.... People growing up in different countries copy their parents and believe in the God or gods of their own country. These beliefs cannot all be right.

If one of them is right, why should it be the belief that you happen to have inherited in the country that you were born? You do not have to be very sarcastic to think something like this: "Isn't it remarkable that almost every child follows the same religion as their parents, and it always just happens to be the right religion?".'

If the young Dawkins had twigged that religion is the performance of faith, then perhaps he would have asked a different question. Isn't it strange that we respond to our sense of God in so many different ways?

It is a question that Dawkins more directly addressed in his work as an evolutionary biologist.

The Selfish Gene

Before Dawkins became famous as an atheist, he was famous as a scientist, albeit an atheist one. His 1976 book, *The Selfish Gene*, was voted the 'most inspiring science book of all time' in a poll carried out by the Royal Society in 2017, beating Darwin's *On The Origin of the Species* into third place.

In the grand scale of things, the book may be a mere embroidery of the theory of evolution that Darwin proposed in his book, but it is clear why it won the poll. *The Selfish Gene* turns evolution into something personal. It is a direct challenge to who we think we are.

Before and after the publication of *On the Origin of the Species* we were able to think of ourselves as single living entities comprising of a mind and a body with a common purpose and a limited lifespan. *The Selfish Gene* brings all that into doubt. Are we one thing? Or two: our genes and our selves? What do we mean by life when it can all be explained so mechanically? Where is the distinction between our minds and our bodies, when so much of our behaviour is genetically programmed? To what extent do we have a common purpose with our genes when their intent seems so much more selfish than our own? What is the meaning of death when our genes may live on for millennia?

Dawkins give his explanation of what he thinks we are in the preface to the book. 'We are survival machines — robot vehicles blindly programmed to preserve the selfish molecules known as genes.'[94] It brings to my mind the image of Tony Stark in his Iron Man suit in the Marvel Cinematic Universe. Except that in this version, Tony Stark isn't a billionaire inventor. He is a strand of carbon, nitrogen, oxygen, phosphorous and hydrogen atoms, bonded together in a helical molecule. This molecule has developed two superpowers: the ability to replicate itself, and a superhuman instinct for survival. That is why he created the robotic suit on which it now habitually relies. As a single twist of DNA floating in the primeval soup, four million years ago it was vulnerable. After millions of replications, slight imperfections in the process led to versions of our molecular Tony Stark being created with casings to protect themselves from the environment. After millions more iterations, these casings grew in variety and sophistication. Today there are at least 8.7 million suits in our molecular Tony Stark's Hall of Armoury. Each suit represents a species with a unique set of special powers.

These suits are programmed to have characteristics (i.e. legs, leaves, cell walls, etc.) and behaviours (i.e. migrating across continents, aggression against male rivals, nurturing the young) by our genes. The main thesis of *The Selfish Gene* is that this programming has happened entirely as a result of the ruthless determination of individual genes to survive and replicate.

This is an important point from a science point of view. It had previously been thought that groups, rather than genes, were the units of natural selection. The theory of group selection was based on the idea that animals often appear altruistic. For example, parents often nurture their young at the expense of themselves. Honeybees often find themselves giving their lives to protect the swarm because they are designed to die after they sting. Birds living in flocks will often put themselves at risk by sounding alarm calls when a predator approaches.

The Selfish Gene shows how these and every other aspect of animal behaviour might be explained by the selfish interests of genes. For example, genes that favour parents nurturing the young are likely to be favoured in natural selection in animals where the young are helpless at birth. Genes want the bodies they inhabit to survive to maturity so that they can reproduce. Genes that encourage worker bees to go on suicide missions against potential hive invaders are likely to be selected over those which don't, because worker bees are infertile. Their DNA is passed on by the queen whom they will be prepared to die to protect. Bird calls and other communications between animals may also have a net benefit to the genes of the individual if their safety is dependent on the behaviour of others in their flock or pack. Dawkins even comes up with an explanation of why praying mantis genes might be OK with the risk that the female of the species might bite off and consume the head of the male during sex. It seems the male can transfer their sperm well enough without a head, and the female can use the extra meal to help feed the eggs which will in fact be fertilised posthumously from the male's stored sperm.

There are still some instances where altruism cannot be explained purely in terms of the benefit to an individual gene, however Dawkins points out that the beneficiaries are almost always close relatives. For example, baby chicks feed in clutches following their mother. When they find something tasty they give a short melodious twitter which summons their siblings to join the feast. This might sound like altruism on the part of the chick that finds itself sharing its meal. In fact, it can be explained as the selfishness of genes in action. Those sharing the meal are full siblings. The chick shares enough DNA with them for it to be genetically worth sharing the meal with them.

Where we start to see behaviours which can't be explained by selfish genes is when we switch our attention to humans. We have a unique ability to override the selfish impulses of our genes. For example, we do not tend to eat our stepchildren as male lions do. They might be tasty. Eating them would also get them out the way, leaving more resources for one's own children. We don't behave like that because of culture. In the past various human societies practised cannibalism, but today the practice is an almost universal taboo. The transmission of culture has enforced that taboo. Humans are able to share ideas between each other in a way that animals are not.

Dawkins sees in culture a powerful new rival to the gene. It seems to spread by making copies of itself in the same way that genes do. He invented the word 'meme' to explain how it works:

'A new kind of replicator has recently emerged on this very planet. It is staring us in the face. It is still in its infancy, still drifting clumsily in its primeval soup, but it is already achieving evolutionary change at a rate that leave the old gene panting far behind.

The new soup is the soup of human culture. We need a name for the new replicator, a noun that conveys a unit of cultural transmission or unit of imitation. "Mimeme" comes from a suitable Greek root, but I want a monosyllable that sounds a bit like "gene".'[95]

Memes have the upper hand over genes because they can spread more rapidly around the world than genes. In the Tony Stark/Iron Man analogy it means that the software in the robotic suit has taken on a life of its own and now moves in ways our molecular Stark is unable to control. It uses contraception.

It likes art and music. It lives in blended families and same sex arrangements, as well as units that be explained by the selfishness of our genes.

Dawkins sees the rise of the meme as a reason to see hope in humanity. The original edition of *The Selfish Gene* concludes with the words: 'We are built as gene machines, and cultured as meme machines, but we have the power to turn against our creators. We, alone on earth, can rebel against the tyranny of the selfish replicators.'

In this analysis, religious faith exists as a meme or complex of related memes. Dawkins is worried about how successful the so called 'God meme' has been at spreading itself. Does this almost universal success imply that that human brains have evolved to be particularly receptive to it? He doesn't think so. Instead, he argues that memes don't have to rely on genes to spread. Religion's persistence can be explained by its psychological appeal alone. It provides a 'superficially plausible answer to deep and troubling questions about existence'. It suggests injustices in this world can be rectified in the next.

'Hellfire,' he declares, 'might almost have been planned deliberately by a Machiavellian priesthood trained in deep psychological indoctrination techniques'.[96]

He also identifies the blindness of faith as a similarly effective part of the religious meme complex: 'Blind faith can justify anything. If a man believes in a different god, or even if he uses a different ritual for worshipping the same god, blind faith can decree that he should die — on a cross, at the stake, skewered on a Crusader's sword, shot in a Beirut street, or blown up in a bar in Belfast. Memes for blind faith have their own ruthless ways of propagating themselves'.

Dawkins feels that faith is also a weakness in the religious meme complex. In a footnote explaining the spread of scientific memes he says: 'Some scientific ideas are actually right, others wrong! Their rightness or wrongness can be tested; their logic can be dissected. They are really not like pop-tunes, religions or punk hairdos'.[97]

It seems to imply that Dawkins believes that truth rather than psychological effectiveness is the long-term arbiter of the success of a meme. And the long term for a meme may turn out to be a lot longer than the long term for a gene. Over time, genes are steadily dissolved into the common pool, but memes may survive in a recognisable form for centuries. For example, the ancient Greek philosopher, Socrates, may or may not have a gene surviving to this day, but his meme complex is still going strong.

The Selfish Gene meme is such a striking one that it should ensure its survival in the meme pool for many centuries as well. But that is not Dawkins' only objective in his writing. It is not enough that his memes should thrive. He wants to see the God meme disappear. That is his purpose in writing *The God Delusion*.

Finding God in The Selfish Gene

So how can God grow out of *The Selfish Gene*? It doesn't leave much space for the divine. Dawkins reduces the world into two main actors: genes (which are molecules) and memes (which are essentially ideas). Together these two four-letter nouns can explain all of life and human behaviour. It is a great feat of simplification. Many would say over-simplification, but let's not argue about that. What I think is interesting is that the methodology Dawkins uses to reach this conclusion reveals something quite unexpected. It reveals the signature of the divine.

How so?

Much of the science behind *The Selfish Gene* grows out of what is known as game theory. This is a branch of mathematics has become the most important way in which behaviour modelled in biology and the social sciences. It makes the assumption that all interactions between people (and indeed between all living things) are essentially games with scores. Players should be expected to aim for the high score. Some games (like chess) are known as zero sum games; there is a winner and a loser. If the winner scores +1 and the loser scores -1, then if you add the two results together you get zero. In other games (like roulette) there is the possibility that more than one person can win. Typically, these games involve a non-playing banker who pays when the losers outnumber the winners. One particular zero sum game — the Prisoner's Dilemma — has become the basis of behavioural science.

The game gives two players two options: either cooperate (c) or defect (d). This creates four possible outcomes (c/c, c/d, d/c and d/d) in which different scores can be awarded according to the choices made. The original scenario had two prisoners being interrogated about a crime in separate cells. Both know that the police will fit them up for a lesser crime if they both keep quiet, but if either one of them talks while the other keeps mum, the one who talks will be let off scot-free while the other gets a long prison sentence. If they both inform on each other they will both get time off the long sentence (but they will still have to spend more time in jail than they might have if they had both kept quiet). Game theory suggests that it is in both prisoners' best interest to talk to the police. That is because the best that can happen if they talk is better than the best that can happen if they stay silent, and the worst that can happen if they talk is also better than the worst that can happen if they keep quiet.

Much of evolutionary biology is based on modelling interactions between organisms as non-zero sum games. The approach was pioneered by one of Dawkins' major influences, John Maynard Smith. He used a game of hawks and doves to illustrate the concept of an "evolutionarily stable strategy". It works as follows:

A species in a territory can have one of two possible strategies:

- Hawk, which involves fighting whoever they encounter until they win or are seriously injured; and,
- Dove, which involves backing down avoiding fights wherever possible.

When two hawks meet, they tear each other apart until there is an eventual winner. When two doves meet, neither does any harm to the other. However, when a dove meets a hawk, the hawk wins, but the losses of the dove are not critical.

Maynard Smith used this game to show that neither an all-dove nor and all-hawk strategy was stable in the long term. Each were liable to invasion by the other. A community of doves would thrive until a hawk arrived on the scene and started intimidating them and seizing their resources. A community of hawks would be such a bloodbath that a dove could slip in and do rather better than all the injured hawks. In both cases you would expect an eventual equilibrium to be achieved between the hawks and doves. Any more hawks would be a disadvantage to the hawks because of the increased risk of injury and any more doves would be a disadvantage to the doves because the increased risk of conflict with hawks. Maynard Smith called this equilibrium the Evolutionarily Stable Strategy (ESS). It is defined as a strategy that cannot be improved upon by a better mutant strategy entering the population. Using game theory to establish that a genetic strategy is evolutionarily stable is one of the most important ways that evolutionary biologists look to validate their hypotheses.

Dawkins added an extra chapter to *The Selfish Gene* in the 30th Anniversary Edition, to discuss an elaborate non-zero sum game he had devised with the US political scientist, Robert Axelrod, during the 1980s. It models behaviour in an iterative way to determine whether altruism or competition is the best strategy. The findings are quite remarkable.

Players have a choice of collaborating or defecting in one-on-one interactions. There are four possible outcomes:[98]

- You both cooperate and you both get three progeny (i.e. replications of your strategy) going through to the next round.
- You defect and the other player cooperates, and you get five progeny going through to the next round (the other player gets none).
- You cooperate, the other player defects and you get no progeny going through to the next round (the other player gets five).
- You both defect and get one progeny going through to the next round.

In the traditional, one-round game of prisoners' dilemma both players acting rationally should defect. This evolutionary version of the prisoner's dilemma led to the opposite conclusion. I will list the main findings here under my own headings.

1. **The nice shall inherit the earth**. The strategies that were initially fed into the game were submitted by 63 game theorists around the world. Axelrod divided these strategies into nice and nasty strategies. Nice strategies were defined as those which never defected first. Nasty strategies were those which defected without provocation. For example 'always cooperate' is a nice strategy, but so is 'tit-for-tat', because it is never the first to defect, although it will punish the other side by defecting for one round if the other side defects first. Nasty strategies include 'always defect' and 'prober' strategies which randomly defect to cash in on the additional progeny you

get for defecting when the other side tries to cooperate. What Axelrod discovered was that after around 1000 generations the nasty strategies had all been squeezed out. The entire game was dominated by nice strategies that repeatedly played cooperate, with tit-for-tat being the most dominant.

2. **Saints are not of this world, but their time will come.** Despite its success 'tit-for-tat' is not an evolutionarily stable strategy because once it dominates the population it is liable to be invaded by players playing more saintly strategies such as 'always cooperate'. 'Always cooperate' is not a successful strategy in earlier rounds because it always gets wiped out by nasty strategies.

3. **Darkness shall not overcome the light.** The equilibrium that is eventually reached in the game depends on the starting position. If there is a critical mass of 'nasty' strategies being played, then the nice won't inherit the earth. Those players following an 'always defect' strategy will end up dominating the game. That is because a player playing a nice strategy in a sea of players pursuing nasty strategies will steadily lose until they are eliminated. The exception is if there is a small cluster of players pursuing nice strategies in a sea of nastiness. In those circumstances the 'nice' players will interact enough with each other to grow their population despite the losses they make in their interactions with 'nasty' players. Eventually the cluster will grow enough to squeeze out the darkness. The reverse is not true of a cluster of players pursuing a nasty strategy in a sea of players pursuing a nice strategy. Their relative rate of growth from interaction with each other cannot keep pace with the much faster rate of growth that the 'nice' players get from interacting with each other. The light overcomes the darkness.

4. **It is divine to forgive**. Axelrod also categorised strategies between those that held grudges (i.e. those which remembered and punished defection long after the offence) and those which forgot a defection quickly. Forgiving strategies included tit-for-tat, tit-for-two-tats (i.e. a strategy that allows the opponent to defect twice before the player defects in retaliation). What he discovered was that forgiving strategies were, in the long run, much more successful than those which bore grudges.

5. **The green-eyed monster will lead you to hell**. Dawkins remarks that in practice real people don't pursue the successful 'nice' strategies recommended by Axelrod's experiments. That is because we hate to see other players doing better than ourselves. We are inclined to defect, not because we want to do well, but because we want our opponents to do badly. Nice strategies rarely win a round because winning involves defecting when the other player is trying to cooperate.

6. **Love your neighbour as yourself**. If you count up the combined scores (i.e. progeny) of each possible outcome, you can see that it heavily favours cooperation:

   - Both players cooperate: six progeny
   - One player cooperates, other defects: five progeny
   - Both players defect: two progeny

   It means that the best strategy is not to aim to win as an individual, but to cooperate to maximise the overall number of progeny. Dawkins suggests that the players should link arms and laugh all the way to the bank. Another way of putting it is that if we think of others before ourselves, everyone will do better.

7. **Believe in eternal life**. If a game has a finite number of rounds, then it always pays to defect on the final round. That is because there is no chance of being punished for defection and so the upside outweighs the downside. The same logic means that it probably pays to defect on the penultimate round as well, given that the outcome of the final round is decided. A belief that the end is final paves the way to a hell of non-cooperation.

I added my own headings to the conclusions that Dawkins and Axelrod draw from their evolutionary version of the prisoners' dilemma. I think the point that I am trying to make should be obvious: game theory strongly favours a religious world view. It is an evolutionarily stable strategy.

Sidebar: Consciousness versus the Selfish Gene

The selfish gene is not consciously selfish in Dawkins' telling. It just appears selfish because the way natural selection favours the fittest genes in each generation makes them appear intolerant of weakness and determined to succeed. It is not totally clear whether Dawkins believes that consciousness even exists. When asked directly about his attitude towards consciousness in a debate with the former Archbishop of Canterbury, he is honest about his confusion. 'One could programme a computer exactly as though it were conscious, so it could pass the Turing Test,[99] and actually fool people into thinking it was conscious, but I would still have trouble believing that it actually would be, and yet I think I have to be committed to the idea that it would be.'[100]

His squeamishness about the concept of consciousness seems to reflect the fact that he considers the evolution of consciousness as 'the most profound mystery facing modern biology'.[101] Dawkins can see why imaginative self-awareness might be genetically useful: it gives us the ability to simulate the possible outcomes of an action, without having to learn through trial and error. What he can't understand is the process by which it might have emerged.

At the heart of the problem is the fact that we can't measure consciousness. In fact the only thing that we can be fairly sure is conscious is ourselves. This opens the door to philosophy. It is where the polymath psychiatrist, Iain McGilchrist (see previous sidebar 'Uniting the Brain') comes in. He uses the confusion over the nature of consciousness to turn the theory of evolution on its head. In *The Matter with Things*, McGilchrist writes: 'Consciousness is nothing to our purpose; we are to the purpose of consciousness'.[102] He argues that instead of life on earth evolving blindly as a result of the accidental creation of a self-replicating molecule, the whole thing is driven by consciousness. The universe is driven by a will to realise itself in its fullest form.

This idea has a nice resonance with Friedrich Nietzsche's idea that every living thing is driven by a desire for self-realisation that we discussed in Chapter 1. Except that McGilchrist has a much bigger vision of this life force that the German philosopher. He does not attempt to draw an evolutionary line between conscious organisms and unconscious ones. Instead, he attributes consciousness to the whole of life, and raises the possibility that consciousness is both divided between each of us but also part of a universal whole. It is from here that we get our sense of the sacred, McGilchrist argues.

It is difficult for scientists like Dawkins to stand in McGilchrist's way. Without the ability to measure consciousness, or describe the physical process that creates it, they have to allow McGilchrist to run ahead. As he does so he gathers them into his grand theory, arguing that the process of science itself is part of consciousness's purpose. Then he comes out with his next big revelation: that our concept of value is not just a by-product of evolution. It, too, is part of this encounter between life and existence that we call consciousness. The things we value — beauty, truth and goodness — are therefore not just the discoveries of consciousness, but its objective.

McGilchrist is not a Christian; he identifies more closely with Taoism. However, his work is an inspiration to all religious people. It pushes back against scientific materialism to make space for God as the consciousness of the universe. As someone who has spent his career studying the function of the brain, he associates the loss of sense of the divine in our society with the growing prominence of left brain thinking in our culture. The left brain is responsible for linear reasoning, precise language, and detailed analysis. According to McGilchrist, it struggles to understand the big picture, but is confident enough to pretend that it does.

'The prevailing account of a meaningless and purely material cosmos, supplied by the reductionist strategy of the left hemisphere, fails to make sense of value, whether that be truth, goodness or beauty, just as it fails to make sense of consciousness. Its answer in every case is the same: that they must be emanations of that purely material cosmos ... that exist purely to further utility.'[103]

McGilchrist singles out Dawkins' world view out as an example of this kind of left brain thinking. However, he does propose a compromise, writing: 'I would love to build a bridge to Richard Dawkins and his like here. Would they be willing to consider a description of nature as being something that discovers what it is in the process of becoming what it is and the point and process of which lies in itself: a free exuberant creation, not a micro-controlled one? No algorithm, not robots, no programme. Just an endless self-discovering act of creation'.[104]

What Is the Big Idea?

The God Delusion doesn't have a big idea in the sense that *The Selfish Gene* has a big idea. What it has is a missionary zeal for atheism that had never been expressed so effectively in writing before. Dawkins' humour, his sense of morality, and his curiosity ensure that he is likeable — and persuasive — as a narrator. Dawkins is nowhere offensive to religion. Nothing he says is obviously untrue or evil. It is this very agreeableness that makes *The God Delusion* a difficult read for a Christian.

Christian values such as goodness and truth are his values too, but he sets them up in opposition to Christian practices that seem to be quite the reverse. Naturally you find yourself rooting for Dawkins against the bigots and blockheads on the other side.

In the penultimate chapter of the book, for example, he tells the story of the kidnapping of Edgardo Mortara. Edgardo was 6 years old and living with his Jewish parents in Bologna when, in 1856, he was legally seized by the papal police acting under orders from the Inquisition. 'Edgardo was forcibly dragged away from his weeping mother and distraught father to the Catechumens (house for the conversion of Jews and Muslims) in Rome, and thereafter brought up a Roman Catholic. Aside from brief visits under close priestly supervision, his parents never saw him again,'[105] Dawkins reports.

What did Edgardo do to deserve this?

He was secretly baptised by a Christian house servant. 'It was a central part of the Roman Catholic belief-system that, once a child had been baptised, however informally and clandestinely, that child was immediately transformed into a Christian.' By law the Church had the right to remove the boy from his parents to bring him up under its care.

Nobody reading a story like that wants to be on the side of the Church. You have to share Dawkins' outrage. The trouble is that you must then decide whether you want to share his conclusion: 'This nineteenth century human tragedy sheds a pitiless light on present-day religious attitudes towards children'.

I am not sure that it does.

Rather, it makes me wonder if most of *The God Delusion* should be read as a diatribe against the abuses of the Church. It could be a modern-day equivalent of the *Ninety-Five Theses* which Martin Luther nailed to the door of the castle church of Wittenberg in 1517.

The Anti-Luther

Read this quote from American anti-abortion activist Randall Terry, which Dawkins brings up in a discussion of what he calls the American Taliban:

'I want you to let a wave of intolerance wash over you. I want you to let a wave of hatred wash over you. Yes, hate is good ... Our goal is a Christian nation. We have a Biblical duty, we are called by God, to conquer this country. We don't want equal time. We don't want pluralism. Our goal must be simple. We must have a Christian nation built on God's law, on the Ten Commandments. No apologies.'

Dawkins wants us to read this as just another example of the bigots and blockheads aligned on the side of religion. He treats it as evidence that there is a strain of fascism in the American Christian right which would dearly like to set up a theocracy. I find it impossible to read it like that. I hope that most other Christians would do as well. The most obvious reading of it is that Randall Terry is not a Christian. Or at least he is not a Christian as might be defined as someone who tries to follow the teachings of Jesus.

This observation seems to go to the heart of the crisis I mentioned in the introduction to this book. Christianity lives on a burning platform. It is being consumed by identity politics at one end and atheism at the other. The space between the anti-Christianity of Terry and the anti-Christianity of Dawkins is getting narrower. The odd thing is that Dawkins seems to have a stronger sense of Christian morality than Terry, while Terry can claim to have a stronger Christian faith than Dawkins.

In fact, you could see Dawkins as the anti-Luther. *The Ninety-Five Theses* were written as a polemic against the sale of indulgences. Indulgences offered the people who paid for them a fast track to heaven by reducing the amount of time they might have to spend in purgatory as a result of their sins. Luther argued that this was a corruption of Christ's message. He asserted that Christians could not achieve salvation through good works. They were saved on the basis of their faith alone. It became one of the five pillars of Protestantism (the Catholic Church believes that salvation is though faith *and* good works).

Dawkins' main concern is about the combination of faith and bad works. He thinks that the one follows the other, regardless of the denomination. For example, he quotes from the letters sent to Einstein after he wrote a paper explaining why he did not believe in a personal God. They show a nasty combination of religious bigotry and callousness. 'In the past ten years nothing has been so calculated to make people think that Hitler had some reason to expel the Jews from Germany as your statement,' one correspondent wrote. Another chimed in: 'We will not give up our belief in our God and his son Jesus Christ, but we invite you, if you do not believe in the God of the people of this nation, to go back to where you came from'.

I think that what Luther had not expected, but Dawkins has put his finger on, is that the meaning of faith would steadily change after his death in 1546. Advances in science have proved that many of the assumptions made by the pre-modern Church about the natural world were wrong. It means that the word 'faith' has steadily become more synonymous with 'belief in things that others would consider impossible'.

Dawkins despairs. How can you reason with someone who won't accept reason? The traditional Church of England also despairs. It was built on the Elizabethan theologian Richard Hooker's three-legged stool of scripture, tradition, and reason. Now it finds reason in conflict with faith wherever it turns.

Alice, from Lewis Carroll's *Alice Through the Looking Glass* also despairs: 'There's no use trying,' she said; 'one can't believe impossible things'.

'I daresay you haven't had much practice,' said the Queen. 'When I was younger, I always did it for half an hour a day. Why, sometimes I've believed as many as six impossible things before breakfast.'

If you were to ask Martin Luther what he meant by faith, it would not involve six impossible things before breakfast. Most likely he would have explained it in terms of his trust and confidence in the promises of God. Faith to him would have been a way of expressing the quality of a personal relationship, as these days we might say: 'You will do well, I have faith in you'.

Dawkins' definition of faith doesn't have this element of personal trust. He emphasises its blindness. For him faith is a 'belief in a counterfactual state of affairs'.

I think that the Church can learn from this. We can and should ask ourselves more searching questions about the nature of faith, when we see such terrible things being done in its name. We can learn from Dawkins because he doesn't have to perform faith when he talks about faith. He is an atheist and not subject to faith's quantum dynamics.

The God Delusion could help make a better Church in the twenty-first century in the same way that Luther's *Ninety-Five Theses* helped drive out venality and corruption from the Catholic Church in the sixteenth century. I will use the language of evolutionary biology to explain why.

The Game Theory of Belief

One might model the way that the trust and confidence definition of faith has interacted with the 'impossible beliefs' definition of faith in a similar way to Maynard Smith's modelling of Hawk and Dove populations above. We might imagine an initial religious population would be dominated by a 'St Francis' meme. This values quiet faith, humility, and good deeds. If there are atheist memes in the meme pool, they are quiet and non-threatening. Then a new religious meme enters the population. In some ways the new meme mimics the St Francis meme; both appear to talk about the same God. However, the reproductive mechanism is different. It is noisier (i.e. evangelical) and more polarising (i.e. socially conservative) than the St Francis meme. I will call it 'Rapture' because many of those who share the meme believe that they will be taken up to heaven imminently. Its noisiness means that it moves across the meme pool much quicker than the St Francis meme. However, this speed does not mean that it quickly dominates the meme pool. Its interactions are polarising; each one creates at least as many noisy atheists (let's call them Dawkins) as it converts to Rapture. This is not a problem because Rapture has a strange symbiotic relationship with the Dawkins meme. A cluster of the Rapture meme will draw strength by being surrounded by Dawkins; it likes to feel embattled in godless world. Similarly, a cluster of Dawkins will draw strength from being surrounded by Rapture; Dawkins needs religion to be obnoxious to survive.

What does this mean for the long-term outlook of St Francis in the meme pool? It is not noisy enough in distinguishing itself from either Rapture or Dawkins to compete with either. Furthermore, it doesn't impose bad enough exit penalties on members leaving to slow its decline.

Yet I see good reason to be optimistic for St Francis in the long term. Both of its opponents are liable to be infiltrated by mutant memes that make them more vulnerable to St Francis.

Rapture is vulnerable to invasion by a political nativist meme — let's call it Trump — that mimics Rapture with a noisy support for counterfactual beliefs and political nativism, but shares none of its Christian values. As it spreads it creates an opportunity for the quiet goodness of the St Francis meme.

Dawkins is vulnerable to a scientific fundamentalist meme — let's call it AI — that fails to recognise the value of human authenticity. This new meme feeds off the same excitement around technology that the Dawkins meme did, but it has no misgivings about whether machines can replicate consciousness and it doesn't see the importance of ineffable human things such as music and the beauty of nature. As it spreads, it creates an opportunity for the St Francis meme which feeds on the mysteries of humanity.

Science and Religion

Dawkins' dream is that science will eventually explain everything. In *The God Delusion* he quotes Einstein as saying: 'To sense that behind anything that can be experienced there is a something that our mind cannot grasp and whose beauty and sublimity reaches us only indirectly and as a feeble reflection, this is religiousness. In this sense I am religious'. Dawkins then adds: 'In this sense I too am religious, with the reservation that "cannot grasp" does not have to mean "forever ungraspable"'.[106]

Einstein's definition of God seems good to me (where we differ is on whether this God can be personal). I suspect that the vast majority of people equally believe in the existence of something ungraspable behind what we can experience. Only a minority would accept Dawkins' belief that science will eventually explain everything. That is what makes Dawkins' atheism so vulnerable in the meme pool.

The metaphor Dawkins uses for the impact of science is the widening of the slit in a burka (i.e. the form of hijab popular in Afghanistan which covers the whole body, sometimes leaving only a thin gauze for the wearer to see the world through). 'Our eyes see the world through a narrow slit in the electromagnetic spectrum,' he suggests. Visible light is just a chink of light in a vast dark spectrum; science broadens the scope of our vision, and will eventually enable us to see everything.[107]

I would use a different metaphor. Science is like a flame in a cave. As it burns more brightly, we begin to realise the enormous dimensions of the cave: soaring lofts, complex side chambers with murky currents flowing who knows where, and the shadows of distant passages too numerous to be explored. The flame turns our initial perception of being confined in a limited space on its head. We discover that we are uncovering the infinity of God.

Faith is the question of our relationship with this infinity. It is not the bucket of water that douses the flame.

Where Is God in *The God Delusion*

When we came to talk about *The God Delusion* with the youth discussion group at the University Church, I found myself doing most of the talking. That is because *The God Delusion* is much more directly and challengingly atheist than other books we covered. It raises a lot of questions to which these teenagers wanted answers.

One of them, Marion, has already read it.

What did she think?

'I don't think it is really about our kind of Church,' she replies.

'He seems to think that Christians must believe in the creation and hate gay people. He seems to take the Bible very literally. It is like he is trying to find bits of Christianity that are obviously wrong and then saying that the whole lot must be wrong as a result.'

I agree, but doesn't she also think that he makes some good points?

She doesn't answer but continues with her own line of thought: 'What I don't know is what we are supposed to believe in this Church. I know we have the creed, but sometimes I think we just say the words.'

'Yes,' says Rosamond joining the conversation. 'I always wonder about that too. When it says Jesus became incarnate of the Virgin Mary does that mean we believe in the virgin birth or is that just the Catholics?'

'What about "seated at the right hand of the Father"? Is it like we have to believe there are chairs in Heaven?' Harry suggests, trying a little too obviously to derail the conversation.

I say that I think we need to get back to Dawkins. My point about him is that he seems to think that faith is about believing that impossible things are true, like Jesus and God are sitting in chairs in Heaven somewhere. In my view, faith is really about having trust and confidence in the promises of God expressed through Jesus.

'How do you mean?' asks George. He is the most serious of the group and wants to move the conversation on.

I say that before I start to explain, I should make two things clear. First that I am not a good Christian: I don't live up to what I think. Second, that my way of thinking always changes over time. That seems to be part of the nature of these things. It is difficult to reach a final certainty. At the moment, I think that Christian faith is made up of two parts. The first is about God. It is about being receptive to the idea that there is more to the world than we can easily understand, and opening our mind to the possibilities that that might entail. It is about refining our sense of wonder to reach out to this thing. This is what religious faith is most generally about. The message I get from Dawkins is that the moment we think we have reached certainty, this God dies. That is because when people start thinking that they have the monopoly on truth, they start doing bad things. Once you think you have the power of God behind you, what is there to stop you? *The God Delusion* is a good way of reminding people to approach religion with humility.

The second part is what I would call the 'big pearl'. This is the idea that the life of Jesus, and his message of love and self-sacrifice, explains what the nature of our relationship with this incredibly abstract God should be. I call it the 'big pearl' after the parable of the merchant who finds a pearl of great price and then sells everything to own it. This part of faith is about accepting the fundamental importance of Jesus' message and trying to live by it.

I think when you read *The God Delusion* you can see that Dawkins agrees with most of Jesus' message. What he disagrees with is the impossibility of it all.

'What do you mean by that?' Marion asks.

I think that what Dawkins is trying to say is: 'Us atheists are better at doing good in the world than you Christians. All your crazy beliefs are just an excuse to behave badly'. I think there is a lot of sense in that. I don't think that believing in impossible things makes you a better Christian.

'So does that mean that you don't believe in miracles?' Harry asks, suddenly taking a more serious interest in the conversation.

Not for their own sake, I reply. Dawkins talks about some of the miracles Jesus allegedly did in the Infant Gospel of St Thomas which didn't make it into the Bible. In one of them the child Jesus makes sparrows out of clay that he finds in the bottom of a stream. When he gets caught and told off for working on the Sabbath, he commands them to fly away, and they do. I came across a similar Sufi story[108] once — these are stories told by Islamic mystics — but it had a different punch line. When Jesus makes the birds fly away one of his friends turns to him and says 'Wow! That's a miracle!' Jesus is unimpressed. 'No it isn't,' he says. 'It has no meaning.' If you look at all the miracles in the New Testament, all of them are metaphors for Jesus's gift to the world. They are about feeding us, healing us, and giving us sight. That is the way I understand the miracles.

'So you are saying that the miracles didn't happen?' Harry is not letting this go.

No, I say. What I am saying is that they are stories in the Bible and their message is more important than what actually happened.

'So they didn't happen? What about the resurrection?'

I say I am not sure what happened there either, but that is not the point. The important thing is that the life of Jesus explains our relationship with God.

I can see that I am losing my audience. They want magic, but all I am offering is prevarication.

'What do you think happens when you die?' asks Freya. She too wants magic.

I say that I don't know. I tell them that my father died a few years ago. He had lung cancer, but even before he was diagnosed his personality started to change. He became more and more anxious. In the last two or three months this anxiety almost paralysed him. You could barely have a conversation with him without him getting into a cycle of despair. When he finally died, I started to wonder about eternal life. It just doesn't seem to make sense. Life is fluid. You change continually through your life. Which version of my father would live on? Would it be that old man paralysed with anxiety, or the pessimistic, but playful and incredibly loving one I knew for most of my life? Or perhaps the one I never knew. He came to Oxford on a Rhodes scholarship then returned to colonial Southern Rhodesia to go into politics but left in disgust when the White electorate voted against preparing for Black majority rule. He would have been a very different person then.

I thought about it and decided that we can never understand the meaning of eternal life. That it seems to me is the nature of faith. It is about believing that God loves us individually and without limit, and that we should love him and his creation without understanding the purpose.

This personal story seems to have won them over a little.

'Do you think you will meet him again in Heaven?' Freya asks.

I say that I can't know, and that is why I call it faith. It is the idea that somehow, and in an extraordinary way, things will come good even though it doesn't make sense. That is where the confidence and trust in Jesus comes in.

'What about hell?' asks Rowan. His background in an evangelical Church has given him a taste for hellfire. 'What does God do to bad people?'

I say that is also something that we can't know, and we probably shouldn't speculate on. People shouldn't take it on themselves to make God's judgements for him.

Harry then returns: 'You haven't made yourself very clear. Are you saying that you don't need to believe in any miracles to be a Christian?'

I say that the only necessary magic is the belief that the life of Jesus tells us something unique about the nature of God. The other things are not important.

'I don't think Richard Dawkins would be convinced by that,' remarks Marion. 'Also we don't really have an answer to the problem of other religions. They can't all be true.'

I say that I think that the religions that Dawkins has most difficulty with are those which claim exclusive access to Heaven. You have to believe a few impossibilities here, hate a few gay people there, turn right, then right again and there is Heaven straight in front of you. All other routes lead to hell. That makes a multicultural world very difficult.

'You make a joke of it,' says Harry, 'but the liberal Church isn't much better. What is the point of being a Christian if you are going to say that all faiths are the same. Or maybe you are going to say that only religions that allow gay people into Heaven are OK but the others are wrong.'

I ask Harry whether he remembers when he was younger and we made pin-hole cameras in Sunday school.

'Yes,' he says. 'I think so. We put tracing paper on one end of a cardboard loo roll and silver foil over the other. It didn't really work unless you pointed it outside where the sun was shining. I remember being really pleased when I got a really blurry image of Radcliffe Square upside down on the tracing paper.'

Can you remember why we made them?

No, he couldn't, and neither could any of the others. I then explain what I was thinking. I had this idea that the whole world was like a big black curtain, and everyone was looking for hope in it, but all they could see was blackness. However, some people found little pin pricks in the black drape, and these pin pricks were like religious revelation. The idea was that each religion gets a different view of the same thing, although it is always pretty blurry and in the case of Christianity, upside down. That's why I thought pinhole cameras were a good idea.

'You had a pretty high expectations of our understanding of theology even then,' remarks Harry's older brother, George. 'I must have been about 7 years old.'

Well does he think it stacks up?

'If you were trying to say that religious faith is a way of seeing, then it sort of make sense, but why don't we then combine all religions into one big religion so we can see as much as possible?'

I say I think that we should learn from other religions, but it is difficult to combine their practices. People express their feelings about God in culturally different ways, but ultimately everyone reaches their own personal view.

'I have been thinking,' says Marion. 'You said faith was a way of seeing. That's the same thing that attracts Dawkins to science. He thinks it is a way of seeing the broader picture. That is what he is getting at in the final chapter of the book when he talks about opening up the slit in the burka. Do you think that means that if Dawkins also understood faith to be a way of seeing, then he probably wouldn't have written *The God Delusion.'*

I say it is a nice idea, but it would be difficult to get him to see it that way. A lot of his readers might. They might wonder who is wearing the burka? Is it those who believe maths and measurement are the only way to understand the world? Or is it those who see broader possibilities both inside ourselves and in the purpose of the universe?

This is why I think that his difficulties with consciousness are so damning for him. He is so dogmatic in this belief that science should be able to be able to explain everything that it makes him close his eyes when he comes across something like consciousness that he can't measure.

I think Dawkins would probably say faith is about seeing things that aren't there, but in reality it is about looking for what really matters. There doesn't have to be anything supernatural about that. The problem for Dawkins is that it works in the opposite way to science. Instead of abstracting and simplifying the world into an equation, looking for what matters is more of a spiritual quest which goes on and on.

'And you think that reading *The God Delusion* will help you get closer to an answer?' asks Harry sceptically.

Absolutely, I say, but our discussion has run out of time.

Conclusion

When I re-read *The God Delusion* in preparation for writing this book, it made me think of the eight mesmerising canvases in the Claude Monet waterlilies series, displayed in the Orangerie Museum in Paris. There is something holy about the depths he has created in paint on the surface of the pond at Giverny. It seems to go to the heart of what I am trying to say about faith being a way of seeing. A dark ultramarine can at one moment be the silhouette of an overhanging tree, and the next its reflection — or perhaps we are actually seeing through the water to the abyss of the bottom of the pond. A cerulean blue can be the soaring afternoon sky, or a rippling glint breaking the mirrored veneer of the pond. The lilies themselves have become abstract shapes floating above, below, within and beyond the pond. The effect is hypnotic as your eye tries to calculate the immeasurable depths of the water and the sky. Yet it is all just paint on a flat canvas. The ultramarine Monet used was a complex sodium aluminium silicate containing sulphur. The cerulean blue was a cobalt stannate. You can describe the paintings in chemical and physical terms, but it would miss the point. In order to enjoy its richness, we must see the world through our imagination.

Faith, in its broadest sense, is about seeing the world through our imagination. This is its reward as well as its hazard. If we can imagine that there is more to life than meets the eye, or which can be measured and modelled by mathematics, our experience of it will be sumptuous and fertile. At the same time, if we become so certain of what we see with our imagination that we become blind to every other possibility, we become a danger to ourselves and those around us.

What it means is that we are never going to get a definitive understanding of the revelation of Christ. Christianity, like other religions, is like an arch without a keystone to join the two vaults. On the one side we reach out to religion because we share the sense that there must be a purpose in the world greater than our own. On the other side religion provides a framework for understanding this purpose that seems to make absolute sense. What is missing is the block of stone which joins the two.

In Christianity the gap in the masonry is the gap between literature and history. The Bible is literature. It was written to address questions of purpose and meaning. It does not establish historical fact. As John Gray remarks in *Seven Types of Atheism*, Christianity is liable to falsification: 'The Victorian Debate between science and religion is best forgotten. A more serious challenge to Christianity comes from History. If Jesus were not crucified and did not return from the dead, the Christian religion would be seriously compromised'.[109]

He is right, but Christianity would also be seriously compromised if the story of Jesus did turn out to be a verifiable historical fact. In the Eucharistic prayer the priest says, 'Great are the mysteries of our faith', to which the congregation replies 'Christ has died, Christ has risen, Christ will come again'. If these mysteries became certainties, they would blind us to everything else. You only have to read *The God Delusion* to see the dangers of this. Quite quickly the Randall Terrys of this world would establish their rule under the ten commandments and start kidnapping Jewish children in order to save their souls.

That is why I think we can read Dawkins' book as we might a Gospel. In John 9, there is a convoluted story about Jesus healing a blind man (it is 877 words long compared to 1446 words for the complete resurrection narrative). When they hear of the miracle, the pharisees accuse Jesus of working on the Sabbath. Jesus remarks: 'I have come into the world for judgement so that those who do not see may see, and those who do see may become blind'. We may think of Dawkins as being spiritually blind, but perhaps he can see something that many of his religious critics do not. He sees the danger that certainty about God would unleash on the world.

Chapter 6

Conclusion: Faith Renewed

Jacques Derrida

Friedrich Nietzsche

Richard Dawkins

Stephen Hawking

So can we read these four great atheist books as Gospels? If so, what do we get out of it? Obviously, none of them offer any new revelation of Christ, but they do offer some 'good news' that enhances our understanding of God. (The word gospel derives from the Old English *gōd* meaning good and *spel* meaning news or story.) The four books do this in the following ways:

Friedrich Nietzsche: *Thus Spoke Zarathustra*
God Is Good

Nietzsche imagines a world without God. It means that you can read the book as a counterfactual. What do we lose if we don't have God? The German philosopher is thorough in his vision: he realises that most people would continue to live as if God did exist. They would still be enslaved to a God-given morality. A small number of enlightened people would, however, see the opportunity to unburden themselves of these vestiges of religion. They could then devote their lives to self-expression. They would become creators of great art. They would live boldly — but alone. Zarathustra's world is one without objectivity. Without a God there is no third party to act as witness to anything beyond one's own perception. Our notions of human connection and justice become subsumed into our will to power. It is a bleak vision. It says to me that our sense of God grows out of the feeling that relations with other people matter in some fundamental way. We are not an island entire of itself, which can find fulfilment in its own self-expression. We are a piece of the continent, part of the main, and our belief in God is an expression of that. God is good because we sense that goodness matters.

If you are looking for a reason why Nietzsche wants to kill God, it is not because He or She is evil. It is because religion has become an expression of power. It makes slaves of us. It booms at us: 'Thou shalt not!' It terrified Nietzsche as a child and it is something that Christians should learn from. Nietzsche says every living organism is driven by a will to power. The only exception was Christ. He lived a life of self-abnegation, unable to be an enemy. Nietzsche says he was the first and only Christian. If Christianity is to be a force for good in the world, we need to learn from that.

Jacques Derrida: *Writing and Difference*
Revelation Is Infinite

The Bible is the easy bit of Christianity. The hard bit is its interpretation. It is what splinters the Church, and Derrida opened the floodgates. He argued that we can never reach a finite meaning of words. Instead, they endlessly defer meaning, never actually reaching a concrete conclusion. God in the Bible is a case in point. He is progressively loaded up with powers and superlatives, but by the last chapter of the book of Revelation we are still left with the sense that the word 'God' is a placeholder for something that we don't understand. What we have are long chains of associations and possible meanings, but not the actual thing called 'God'. Derrida described God as an 'absent presence' in the Bible. For him it meant that belief in God was impossible.

There are three ways in which we can respond to this. Either we can agree with Derrida and give up, or we can disagree with him and say it is all post-structuralist nonsense — of course the meaning of the Bible is clear. Alternatively, we can accept that Derrida might have got it right and that his thinking says something quite profound about revelation. It is supposed to be fluid, confusing and infinite. It is an invitation to engage our imagination every day in the meaning of scripture and the meaning of the world. It doesn't offer the kind of concrete answers that might provide the basis for killing people in religious wars. Instead, revelation becomes a will-o'-the-wisp that engages our curiosity at a distance and invites us to follow.

Stephen Hawking: *A Brief History of Time*
God Is with Us

Most Christians today are prepared to accept that the creation story in the Bible is metaphorical. If science tells them that the most likely explanation of the beginning of things is

The Devils' Gospels

the Big Bang, they will accept that, without showing much interest in the details. The underlying assumption is that God was somehow involved in making the Big Bang happen. We can therefore continue to believe that God created all things. Hawking's book aims to disprove this possibility. *A Brief History of Time* outlines the 'no boundary proposal'. This is an explanation of the beginning of time which did not require a creator or first moved mover to initiate it all. Although the theory has yet to be proved, it does challenge Christians to consider: 'where is God?' As Hawking points out, there is no time or space for God to exist in before the Big Bang. Causality — which provides the basis for both the unmoved mover and first cause arguments for the existence of God — simply doesn't exist in the absence of time. A fall-back position for Christians might be to suggest that God exists in some separate realm of meaning and purpose which does not impinge on the physical world, but somehow directs it. This seems a bit thin.

What I read into *A Brief History of Time* is the possibility that God could be in the universe. In fact, we might imagine that He or She is the whole of existence. It is the most logical answer to the question: why doesn't God show up in physics? It is because He or She *is* physics. He or She is everything; an incredible creative force growing explosively out of timelessness and spaceless-ness. We are part of this force, and we should live our lives in harmony with it and its creations. I should add in the small print that this is not a definitive characterisation of God. It is really just a metaphor for a deity we can never hope to fully understand. Besides closing the gap between science and religion, this understanding of God also closes the gap between religion and environmentalism. It suggests that the commandment to love God encompasses a duty towards the planet.

Richard Dawkins: *The God Delusion*
Faith Is a Way of Seeing

Dawkins wrote *The God Delusion* in a bid to stop people believing in God. It outlines the suffering caused by religion and points out the lack of any empirical basis for belief. He imagines a world of no religion where people can enjoy life and can love each other without fear of some terrible post-mortem punishment. It is a convincing argument, but it becomes clear that his real concern is not with religion *per se*. It is with a particular formulation of faith that says you get to heaven by believing impossible things. The more impossible your beliefs, the better your chances of making it. It is a dangerous formulation. It means that religious believers can do terrible things in the world (e.g. blow up the Twin Towers, assassinate abortion clinic workers, emotionally terrorise family members who disagree with them) in the hopes of a reward in the next life. Dawkins is clearly right about this, but is he right about faith? Is that what it is: an agreement to suspend one's faculties of reason in exchange for a better life after death?

Dawkins' own motivation provides an answer. He talks about how science is about broadening one's view of the world. Faith is the same. It is about looking at the world so as to see what matters. It is a much broader viewpoint than science can offer. It reads the world (and scripture) for its metaphorical truths rather than its physical mechanics. Faith in God is not supernatural in that it requires its adherents to see phantasmagorically. But it is supernatural in that it is receptive to more possibilities in life than can be explained by biology and physics alone.

Escaping the Burning Platform

At the beginning of this book, I described how Christianity was caught between the flames of the culture war and the ice-cold sea of atheism. The culture war — that is to say, the bitter divide between conservatives and progressives in Europe and North America over issues relating to diversity and identity — is destroying Christianity from within. It is turning the faith into an obnoxious political brand which is driving many young people towards atheism.

This conflict is often characterised as a battle between those who believe in so-called universal values (such as human rights, democracy, respect for diversity etc.) and those who believe in the rightness of the cultural values they grew up with. I am not so sure that it is.

In my day job I travel a lot. I have done business all over the world. What I find disturbing in my travels is how much each country's national aspirations run so much against each other. It has become very easy to hate a foreign country. The xenophobia of the left denouncing whole nations for their alleged moral failings is now as strong as the xenophobia of the right, denouncing its enemies on more nativist grounds. I don't think that this is a conflict between universal values and cultural values. It is a stand-off between different brands of tribal morality reinforced by social media algorithms. It is tearing the world apart, not just the Church.

That is the real urgency of the burning platform. The whole world could burn if we get this wrong.

Two things need to happen from a Christian standpoint to avoid a catastrophe. First the Church needs to extract itself from the culture war. Secondly, it needs to make itself relevant enough to end that war. I hope that this book can provide inspiration towards those objectives.

In theory, Christianity should be the perfect antidote to the culture war. The world needs more people who love their enemies, treasure the whole of humanity, and put the interests of others first. In practice, Christianity is right there at the frontline of the conflict creating division. The devils' gospels we have discussed can help extricate the Church from this war.

Nietzsche's book asks Church leaders whether they are driven by power or by love; Derrida's book asks them how they can be so certain of God's revelation. Hawking's book challenges them to consider how God and science can be compatible; Dawkins' book asks them whether faith should make people blind or open their eyes.

If the Church is to be relevant again, it needs to catch up with two centuries of social, scientific and environmental change. Specifically, it needs to be able to provide leadership in a diverse, multi-faith world that is being reshaped by human activity. Each of these things is a challenge to the Church. While Christianity is globally diverse it is locally quite monocultural. For example, at the University Church we are proud of our choral tradition, but it does mean that a tolerance of Thomas Tallis, the sixteenth-century English composer, is a membership requirement. Respect for other faiths has been particularly difficult for the Church. Traditionally other religions were considered fair game for missionary activity, but today Christian universalism is often confused for cultural imperialism or worse, racism. Climate change is another problem for Christianity: its focus on personal salvation leaves little space for planetary salvation. If we are asking ourselves 'what would Jesus do?' about these challenges, we won't find ready answers in the Gospels. They were simply not issues in the first century AD. The argument of this book is that if we are trying to understand the most difficult challenges facing religion, the best place to look for answers is in the writings of those critical of religion. We don't need to agree with their conclusion that God does not exist, but in engaging with their criticisms we can find ways of ensuring that Christianity remains relevant.

The Rebellion

In the chapter on Dawkins' book, *The God Delusion*, I suggested that the evangelical Rapture meme is being replaced by an atheist Trump meme, and the atheist Dawkins meme is being replaced by a scientific fundamentalist AI meme. I also suggested that both the Trump and AI meme were vulnerable to the humble Christianity of the St Francis meme. The reason I am optimistic is because I think people are unhappy with who they are evolving to become, and they are ready for rebellion.

Identity politics is redefining what it means to be human. It divides us up into tribes according to a crude matrix of gender, race, class, age, and religion, and tells us that is all we are. More than that, exacerbated by the tensions between these tribes, it starts to become predictive, telling each tribe how they should think and act. This is reinforced by social media and our online interactions, which similarly reduce and redefine who we are until its categorisation becomes predictive. Among other things it has created a point and click morality in which goodness no longer involves any kind of real-life selflessness. Online there is no virtue. Only virtue signalling.

I think the rebellion against the Trump and AI memes will be driven by a visceral sense that this is not who we are. We are each a unique individual, infinitely subtle and uncategorisable. We don't want to become the people we are online or the people the politicians want us to be, even as we find ourselves steadily becoming them. We want the humble authenticity of the St Francis meme, which despises loud-mouthed virtue signalling. Its goodness is defined by a comprehension of the needs of others and a willingness to put others first.

I think that those who rebel against the Trump meme and the AI meme will not drift back into some kind of apathetic atheism. The rebels will return to the God of St Francis for inspiration. That God also expresses the inexpressibility of humanity in a way that atheism cannot. This is the paradox that I hope has been explained by this book.

If there is one thing that we can learn from atheist writers about God, it is that He or She is not obvious. This is an important fact that religious writers, in their enthusiasm to believe, often skate over. What we get from Nietzsche, Derrida, Hawking and Dawkins over and over again is a reminder of the scientific unbelievability of God. We as Christians should not be afraid to accept this view. It is obviously a feature of Christianity. It is not a bug. We are not *meant* to fully understand Him or Her. We are meant to sense the mystery and be inspired to explore. That mystery is not about an abstract thing called God. It is the mystery of ourselves, our relationship with each other, and our purpose in the universe. It is infinite.

Science is very much part of the exploration of this mystery. Where it goes wrong is where it tries to reduce the world and humanity to a single formula. It is the nature of science to create new wonders, in spite of the intention of scientists. Physicists in pursuit of a simple Theory of Everything instead uncover the beauty and weirdness of quantum mechanics. Biologists, in trying to push forward our understanding of how we are made, find themselves unwittingly adding to the puzzle of our consciousness.

The Other End of History

Most mainstream secular thinkers believe that religion is doomed in the long term. They see an arc of history that stretches from primitive ignorance to modern scientific intelligence. Religious means of regulating community behaviour will eventually be replaced by liberal secular values that offer a reciprocal respect for individual freedoms. The process ought to take us to an eventual 'end of history'. This hasn't come to pass, in part because of the resurgence of religious fundamentalism. Since the terrorist attacks of 9/11, liberalism has struggled with the right to be intolerant. It is an entitlement most regularly claimed by religious groups.

Some liberals see this as a mere bump in the road. They see that the intolerance of a minority is now a powerful driver of the growth of global atheism. They infer from this that religion is still doomed in the long run. Successive generations will be more likely to view religion as a toxic superstition that undermines humanity, and they will abandon it.

There is another narrative that agrees with almost all of this but reaches a very different conclusion. It says that humanity has transformed itself from its primitive initial state to its current state through its ability to build predictive models of how the world works. At the same time there is an awareness that there are aspects of life and the world that can never be modelled. For example, we have a sense of creativity which almost by definition cannot be modelled (i.e. if it works to a formula it cannot be called creative). We also have a yearning for meaning and purpose that is never satisfied by the answers it is given (we always want to ask 'why?' one more time).[110] Most importantly, we have a sense that life itself cannot be created from a model. It might be possible to simulate human responses well enough to confuse someone, but once the mechanism which delivers the simulation is explained, there is no confusion. For example, large language models developed by artificial intelligence provide extraordinarily human responses to questions. However, once one understands the system of probabilities behind such chatbots it is impossible to mistake their intelligence for human intelligence. In the language of quantum mechanics, the wave function collapses.

Historically religion grew out of this sense that while we can understand the world through models, most of what we care about in life cannot be modelled. This created a sense that we can't see the whole picture, that we must be part of something larger than ourselves, and that there is a mystery at the heart of our lives that actually matters. Pre-modern humans looked for divine revelation to help understand this mystery. Many of them found it in the life and teachings of Jesus. These explained that our relationship with the divine (and its relationship with us) is expressed through love. It is a mysterious answer, but it seems to make more sense as we explore it.

During the Enlightenment, the establishment of the empirical method as the basis of predictive science revolutionised our ability to model the world. It revolutionised our ability to make the world work for us. It also changed the way we think about religion. It created the sense that religion should work for us like everything else. Defined inputs would deliver predictable outcomes.

In this grand narrative of history, the growth of atheism was not driven by a better understanding of the physical universe. It was driven by people forgetting the essential mystery of religion — and thinking that it was something that they could work like a piece of machinery. You put faith in at one end and get eternal life out at the other.

The truth is that religion quite fundamentally doesn't work like that. The irony of this book is that it takes a group of atheists to say so.

What I think will reverse the growth of atheism is the realisation that the mysteries that were the original inspiration of religion are not historical curiosities. They actually matter. That is because our ability to make predictive models of the world has moved up a level. We are now in a position where these models are so good at mimicking humanity that it begs the question: 'how are we different from machines?'

After four hundred years of looking at everything with an eye to reduce what we see into its working parts, we will start looking at the world once again for the things that we cannot explain. Instead of asking how they work, we will ask what they mean. That will steadily take us back to God.

Endnotes

1. Sermon reported by Reuters (2022): 'Orthodox Church leader says Russian soldiers dying in Ukraine will be cleansed of sin', 26 September available at www.reuters.com/world/europe/orthodox-church-leader-says-russian-soldiers-dying-ukraine-will-be-cleansed-sin-2022-09-26/.

2. Fox & Friends (2019): Fox News, 9 January.

3. Letter from Benjamin Jowett to Arthur Penrhyn Stanley dated August 15 1858 from Jowett, B. (1899), *Letters*, Abbott, E. and Campbell, L. (eds.). John Murray, London 1899.

4. Baden Powell (sic) was the father of Robert Baden-Powell, the founder of the scouting movement. Powell's wife renamed her children Baden-Powell after his death in June 1860.

5. Powell, B. (1860), 'On the Study of the Evidences of Christianity' in Parker, J. (ed.) *Essays & Reviews*. London, J W Parker & Sons, p.84.

6. Ibid, p.93.

7. Whether this exchange happened on not is subject to some debate (see www.oum.ox.ac.uk/learning/pdfs/debate.pdf).

8. The most detailed reminiscences of the day come from Francis Darwin (1887), a Mrs Sidgwick writing under the pseudonym 'Grandmother' in 1898 and Leonard Huxley (1900).

9. Powell, B. (1860), 'On the Study of the Evidences of Christianity' in Parker, J. (ed.) *Essays & Reviews*. London, J W Parker & Sons, p.125.

10. Letter from Charles Darwin to Baden Powell dated 18 January 1860, available at www.darwinproject.ac.uk/letter/DCP-LETT-2654.xml.

11. Huxley coined the word agnostic in 1869 to describe his attitude towards religion.

12. Nietzsche, F. (1883–5 [1960]), *Thus Spoke Zarathustra* (trans. R. Hollingdale). London, Penguin, p.41.
13. Alcoholics Anonymous' Serenity Prayer.
14. Nietzsche, F. (1883–5 [1960]), p.173.
15. Ibid, p.67.
16. Ibid, p.76.
17. Ibid, p.74.
18. Ibid, p75.
19. Nietzsche, F. (1889 [1998]), *Twilight of the Idols*, (trans. D. Large). Oxford, OUP, p.37.
20. In a letter to Franz and Ida Overbeck, 1889, from Nietzsche, F. (1934), *Werke und Briefe: Historisch-kritische Gesamtausgabe,* (ed. W. Hoppe et al.). Ebenhausen, Langewiesche-Brandt, p.38.
21. Ibid, p.74.
22. Nietzsche F. (1878 [1998]), *Human, all too Human*, (trans. M. Faber). London, Penguin.
23. In a later work (Nietzsche, F. (1895 [1968]), *The Antichrist* (trans. R. J. Hollingdale). Penguin, Middlesex, paragraph 47), Nietzsche explains that God is a 'crime against life' adding: 'If one were to prove this God of the Christians to us, we should be even less able to believe in him.' Although this can be read as an assertion of Nietzsche's atheism, it can also be read as an exploration of the paradoxical nature of God.
24. Nietzsche, F. (1934), p.80.
25. Nietzsche, F. (1862), *Fate and History: Thoughts*. Ebenhausen, Langewiesche-Brandt.
26. Ibid.
27. Letter to Elizabeth Nietzsche, 1865 from Nietzsche, F. (1934).
28. Nietzsche is not wholly consistent in asserting this view. In a later work he suggests that lesser people could be content with religion: 'My philosophy aims at an ordering

of rank: not at an individualistic morality. The ideas of the herd should rule in the herd – but not reach out beyond it,' he writes. Nietzsche, F. (1901 [1968]), *The Will to Power*, (trans. Walter Kaufmann and R.J. Hollingdale). Penguin, Middlesex, p. 162.

29. Paley, C. (2021), *Beyond Bad: How Obsolete Morals are Holding us Back*. London, Coronet.
30. Ibid, p.40.
31. Ibid, pp.90–114.
32. Ibid, p.202.
33. Nietzsche, F. (1883–5 [1960]), p.137.
34. For those who haven't seen the film, it envisages a time when machines have taken over the world. People live simulated lives in virtual reality pods as the Matrix harvests their bioenergy. Morpheus is the leader of the humans working in the real world to overthrow the Matrix. He offers the hero, Neo, a choice of two pills: one (the blue pill) which will allow him to continue to live in the comfortable but illusory world of the Matrix and the other (a red pill) which will awaken him to the grim reality of the war between man and machine.
35. Nietzsche, F. (1883–5 [1960]), p.46.
36. Ibid, p.43.
37. Ibid, p.55.
38. Ibid, p.55.
39. Ibid, p.171.
40. Nietzsche, F. (1908 [1911]), *Ecce Homo*, (trans. A. Ludovici). London, Macmillan p.97
41. Nietzsche, F. (1883–5 [1960]), p.237.
42. Later in life he wrote: 'I do not want life again. How did I endure it? Creating. What makes me stand the sight of it? The vision of the superman who affirms life. I have tried to affirm it myself. Alas.' Quoted in Nietzsche. F. (1920-29), *Collected Works*. Munich, Musarion, Vol XIV.

43. Nietzsche, F. (1883–5 [1960]), p.333.
44. 'The Wanderer and His Shadow', aphorism 204 (1880) from Nietzsche. F. (1920–29), *Collected Works*. Munich, Musarion.
45. Donne, J. (1623), *Devotions upon Emergent Occasions*. Scotts Valley Create Space (this edition 2015) sonnet no.17.
46. Nietzsche, F. (1886 [2003]), *Beyond Good and Evil* (trans. R. Hollingdale). London, Penguin, p.259.
47. Nietzsche, F. (1886 [2018]), *The Antichrist* (trans. by H. Mencken). Durham, Lulu.com, p.112.
48. Ibid, p.93.
49. This assertion requires some qualification. Nietzsche felt connected to the universe on a metaphysical level and he criticised the Christian concept of souls which separate us from each other and the rest of the world, however he felt a deep revulsion towards the influence of other people on our values and behaviour on a psychological level.
50. Nietzsche, F. (1883-5 [1960]), p.91.
51. Mark 16:9; Shorter Ending of Mark NRSV.
52. Matthew 13:13; NRSV.
53. Galatians 3:28 and Galatians 5:1; NRSV.
54. This is not a problem in the Catholic Church where the Pope has ultimate authority over matters of doctrine.
55. Matthew 27:25; NRSV.
56. As ever with Derrida there is an important double entendre here. 'Il n'y pas de hors-texte' (there is no frontispiece) can also be read as 'il n'y a pas dehors texte' (there is no outside text) with the implication that all that exists is text.
57. Hawking, S. (1988), *A Brief History of Time*. London Transworld, p.1.
58. Derrida, J. (1967 [1998]), *On Grammatology* (trans. G. Spivak). London, Routledge, p.41.
59. She is referring to the Oxford Martyrs: Cranmer, Latimer and Ridley who were tried and condemned to death by fire near where the altar in the University Church now stands.

60. 1 Corinthians 13:12; NRSV.

61. Quoted in the introduction of Mountford, B. (2006), *Christianity in 10 Minutes*. Ropley, John Hunt Publishing.

62. Matthew 13:45; NRSV.

63. Hawking, S. (2018), *Brief Answers to the Big Questions*. London, John Murray, p.28.

64. McGilchrist, I. (2009), *The Master and His Emissary: The Divided Brain and the Making of the Western World*. London, Yale University Press.

65. That is not to say that there is not a certain mystery or magic to maths. As Gödel's Incompleteness Theorem suggests, maths cannot be constructed from a defined set of axioms and nor can it prove its own consistency. It means that maths remains an active area of research: its rules change as our understanding advances, but as they do so, they move to eliminate inconsistency and ambiguity.

66. Obviously the scientific consensus changes over time. For example Einstein initially asserted that a Cosmological Constant was necessary to keep the universe from imploding, but subsequently changed his mind and removed it from his field equations of general relativity. More recently the concept has come back into vogue as the energy density of space has become a focus of research. The important point to make is that there is a difference between changing constants so that they better fit empirical data and changing constants without reference to empirical data.

67. Again it is important to stress that science is a work in progress. It only represents objective truth for as long as it is able to predict outcomes. When it disagrees with the empirical data, it ceases to represent objective truth, and incidentally ceases to be science until a better model to explain the data is accepted.

68. McGilchrist, I. (2021), *The Matter with Things: Our Brains, our Delusions and the Unmaking of the World*. London, Perspectiva.

69. Ibid, p.1289.

70. Only things which have no mass such as photons can travel at the speed of light.

71. Hawking, S. and Mlodinow, L. (2010), *The Grand Design: New Answers to the Ultimate Questions of Life*. London, Bantam.

72. Lemaître, G., 'The Beginning of the World from the Point of View of Quantum Theory', in *Nature*, 127 (9 May 1931), p. 706.

73. Carlo Rovelli, 'All being is interaction' from *On Being with Krista Tippett*. On Being Foundation, 2017 from onbeing. org/programs/carlo-rovelli-all-reality-is-interaction.

74. I don't expect the chapter to sway Dawkins himself. He has had more than enough God-botherers trying to save his soul.

75. Gray, J. (2002), *Straw Dogs: Thoughts on Humans and Other Animals*. London, Granta, p.33.

76. Gray, J (2018), *Seven Types of Atheism*. London, Penguin, p.13.

77. Ibid, p.51.

78. Ibid, p.69.

79. Ibid, p.120.

80. Ibid, p.141.

81. Ibid, p.152.

82. Nietzsche, F. (1882[2001]), *The Gay Science* (trans. Josefine Nauckhoff). Cambridge, Cambridge University Press, p.344.

83. 1951 UK census data.

84. 2021 UK census data.

85. Data aggregated from faithsurvey.co.uk.

86. Mamoud, T. (2005), *Multicultural Politics: Racism, Ethnicity and Muslims in Britain*. Edinburgh, Edinburgh University Press.

87. The Congregational Church, the Episcopal Church, the Evangelical Lutheran Church, the Presbyterian Church, the United Methodist Church, the American Baptist Convention, and the Disciples of Christ.

88. Data from churches aggregated by Richard Ostling at getreligion.org.

89. Southern Baptist Convention 2023 report.

90. Data from the Centre for Applied Research in the Apostolate, Georgetown University.

91. I appreciate that the strongest growth in Christianity is in the Global South and that Islam is the fastest growing world religion, but the main focus of Richard Dawkins' book is Christianity in Europe and North America.

92. US Religion Census 2010 and 2020 collated by Ryan Burge.

93. LDS Statistical Report for the 2023 Conference.

94. Dawkins, R. (2016), *The Selfish Gene (40th Anniversary Edition)*. Oxford, OUP, p.xxvii.

95. Ibid, p.249.

96. Ibid, p.257.

97. Ibid, p.426.

98. In the book Dawkins describes three versions of this game, two in which points were awarded at the end of each round and the objective was to maximise the number of points. The third is the version I explain here, where the points are substituted for progeny going through to the next round.

99. I.e. that a human would be unable to distinguish the machine's responses from human responses in a blind test devised by the computing pioneer, Alan Turing.

100. Debate hosted by University of Oxford on 28 February 2012.

101. Ibid, p.76.
102. McGilchrist, I (2022), p.1093.
103. McGilchrist notes that people with right brain injuries often struggle to tell whether something is alive, hence their difficult of understanding consciousness.
104. McGilchrist, I (2022), p.1165.
105. Dawkins, R. (2006), *The God Delusion*. Bantam, London, p.311.
106. Ibid, p.19. It is important to note that this quote continues as follows: 'But I prefer not to call myself [religious] because it is misleading. It is destructively misleading, because for the vast majority of people "religion" implies "supernatural"'.
107. Ibid, p.362.
108. A version of this story can be found in Shah, I. (1973), *Tales from the Dervishes*. London, Panther Books.
109. Gray, J (2018), p.14.
110. The philosopher, Ludwig Wittgenstein, would say that this is a trick of the language, in that it is just grammar which enables us to ask 'why?' questions repetitively. However, it is equally possible that the reason we never reach a satisfactory ultimate answer to 'why?' is because purpose is ultimately mysterious, and its discovery is part of the motivation for living.

THE NEW OPEN SPACES

Throughout the two thousand years of Christian tradition
there have been, and still are, groups and individuals
that exist in the margins and upon the edge of faith. But
in Christianity's contrapuntal history it has often been
these outcasts and pioneers that have forged contemporary
orthodoxy out of former radicalism as belief evolves to engage
with and encompass the ever-changing social and scientific
realities. Real faith lies not in the comfortable certainties of
the Orthodox, but somewhere in a half-glimpsed hinterland
on the dirt track to Emmaus, where the Death of God meets
the Resurrection, where the supernatural Christ meets the
historical Jesus, and where the revolution liberates
both the oppressed and the oppressors.

Welcome to Christian Alternative... a space at the
edge where the light shines through.
If you have enjoyed this book, why not tell other readers
by posting a review on your preferred book site.

Recent bestsellers from Christian Alternative are:

Bread Not Stones
The Autobiography of An Eventful Life
Una Kroll
The spiritual autobiography of a truly remarkable
woman and a history of the struggle for ordination in the
Church of England.
Paperback: 978-1-78279-804-0 ebook: 978-1-78279-805-7

The Quaker Way
A Rediscovery
Rex Ambler
Although fairly well known, Quakerism is not well
understood. The purpose of this book is to explain how
Quakerism works as a spiritual practice.
Paperback: 978-1-78099-657-8 ebook: 978-1-78099-658-5

Blue Sky God
The Evolution of Science and Christianity
Don MacGregor
Quantum consciousness, morphic fields and blue-sky
thinking about God and Jesus the Christ.
Paperback: 978-1-84694-937-1 ebook: 978-1-84694-938-8

Celtic Wheel of the Year
Tess Ward
An original and inspiring selection of prayers combining
Christian and Celtic Pagan traditions, and interweaving
their calendars into a single pattern of prayer for
every morning and night of the year.
Paperback: 978-1-90504-795-6

Christian Atheist

Belonging without Believing
Brian Mountford
Christian Atheists don't believe in God but miss him:
especially the transcendent beauty of his music,
language, ethics, and community.
Paperback: 978-1-84694-439-0 ebook: 978-1-84694-929-6

Compassion Or Apocalypse?

A Comprehensible Guide to the Thoughts of René Girard
James Warren
How René Girard changes the way we think about
God and the Bible, and its relevance for our
apocalypse-threatened world.
Paperback: 978-1-78279-073-0 ebook: 978-1-78279-072-3

Diary Of A Gay Priest

The Tightrope Walker
Rev. Dr. Malcolm Johnson
Full of anecdotes and amusing stories, but the Church
is still a dangerous place for a gay priest.
Paperback: 978-1-78279-002-0 ebook: 978-1-78099-999-9

Readers of ebooks can buy or view any of these bestsellers by
clicking on the live link in the title. Most titles are published in
paperback and as an ebook. Paperbacks are available
in traditional bookshops. Both print and ebook
formats are available online.

Find more titles and sign up to our readers' newsletter at
www.collectiveinkbooks.com/christianity Follow us on
Facebook at https://www.facebook.com/ChristianAlternative